Copycat Recipes

The Easy Guide to The Art of Making Your Favorite

Restaurant Dishes at Home

Talia Gibbs

Tables of Contents

INTRODUCTION 9

CHAPTER 1: HOW TO CREATE THE FEELING OF A RESTAURANT AT HOME 11

CHAPTER 2: COOKING TOOLS NEEDED 13
    APPLIANCES... 13
    COOKING GADGETS 14
    OTHER TOOLS 14
    COOKWARE 15

CHAPTER 3: BASIC INGREDIENTS: REQUIRED 17
    HERBS AND SPICES 17
    SAUCES 18
    BASIC GROCERY ITEMS 19
    BAKING ITEMS.. 19
    FOR DESSERTS.. 20

CHAPTER 4: STORED INGREDIENTS 21
    IN THE REFRIGERATOR.. 21
    IN THE FREEZER 22

CHAPTER 5: HOW TO CHOOSE BEST INGREDIENTS 23
    CHICKEN 24
    MEATS 24
    BEEF 24
    PORK 25
    FISH.. 25
    VEGETABLES 25
    FRUITS 26

CHAPTER 6: COOKING TERMS AND TECHNIQUES THAT ARE MUST KNOW 27
    CUTTING METHODS... 27
    OTHER BASIC CONCEPTS THAT ARE MUST KNOW 28
    FOOD PRESENTATION 29

CHAPTER 7: APPETIZER RECIPES 31
    1. OLIVE GARDEN'S CLAM BRUSCHETTA.. 31
    2. GIRL SCOUT SAMOA COOKIES 33
    3. OLIVE GARDEN'S BRUSCHETTA 35
    4. FAMOUS DAVE'S DRAGON FIRECRACKER CHICKEN WINGS 37
    5. OUTBACK-STYLE SWEET POTATO 39
    6. OLIVE GARDEN STYLE TORTELLINI DO FORNI 41
    7. PEPPERIDGE FARM SAUSALITO COOKIES 43
    8. FAMOUS AMOS CHOCOLATE CHIP COOKIES.. 45
    9. BOSTON MARKET DILL POTATO WEDGES 47
    10. CHILI'S BONELESS BUFFALO WINGS 49
    11. OLIVE GARDENS FRIED MOZZARELLA 51
    12. BENNIGAN'S BROCCOLI BITES... 53

13. RED LOBSTER'S ULTIMATE FONDUE 55

14. MORTON'S STEAKHOUSE SHRIMP ALEXANDER 57

15. RED LOBSTER'S SHRIMP DIABLO 59

16. EMERIL'S NEW ORLEANS'S ROSEMARY BISCUITS 61

17. HARD ROCK CAFÉ'S TUPELO-STYLE CHICKEN 63

CHAPTER 8: SOUP RECIPES 65

1. APPLEBEE'S FRENCH ONION SOUP 65

2. BENNIGAN'S POTATO SOUP 67

3. HUSTON'S WILD RICE AND MUSHROOM SOUP 69

4. OLIVE GARDEN'S ZUPPA TOSCANA 71

5. O' CHARLEY'S BAKED POTATO SOUP 73

6. BRENNAN'S ONION SOUP 75

7. CHILI'S SOUTHWEST CHICKEN CHILI 77

8. BOB EVAN'S CHEDDAR BAKED POTATO SOUP 79

9. GALLAGHER'S CHEDDAR CHEESE SOUP 81

10. HUSTON'S CANADIAN CHEESE SOUP 83

11. MGM GRAND SPICY JAMBALAYA 85

12. OLIVE GARDEN'S ITALIAN SAUSAGE SOUP 87

13. OUTBACK STEAKHOUSE WALKABOUT SOUP 89

14. PANERA BREAD BROCCOLI CHEESE SOUP 91

15. HUSTON'S TORTILLA SOUP 93

CHAPTER 9: SALAD RECIPES 95

1. APPLEBEE'S LOW-FAT BLACKENED CHICKEN SALAD 95

2. FAMOUS DAVE'S SHAKIN' THE SHACK POTATO SALAD 99

3. CHI-CHI'S MEXICAN CHICKEN SALAD 101

4. DAVE AND BUSTER'S STEAK FAJITA SALAD 103

5. GOLDEN CORRAL'S SEAFOOD SALAD 105

6. HUSTON'S GRILLED CHICKEN SALAD 107

7. CHILI'S GRILLED CARIBBEAN CHICKEN SALAD 109

8. APPLEBEE'S SANTA FE CHICKEN SALAD 111

9. CALIFORNIA PIZZA KITCHEN WALDORF CHICKEN SALAD 115

10. LUBY-CAFETERIA'S GREEN PEA SALAD 117

11. DAVE AND BUSTER'S MUFFALETTA SALAD 119

12. CALIFORNIA PIZZA KITCHEN WEDGE SALAD 121

13. KFC BEAN SALAD 123

14. APPLEBEE'S ORIENTAL CHICKEN SALAD 125

CHAPTER 10: MAIN COURSE RECIPES 127

1. APPLEBEE'S SOUTHWEST STEAK 127

2. BOSTON MARKET MEAT LOAF 129

3. CLAIM JUMPER'S ROASTED PORK LOIN 131

4. APPLEBEE'S SANTA FE STUFFED CHICKEN 133

5. BENNIGAN'S SMOTHERED CHICKEN 135

6. OLIVE GARDEN STYLE LASAGNA 137

7. OLIVE GARDEN SPAGHETTI CARBONARA 141

8. OLIVE GARDEN PASTA CON ZUCCHINI 143

9. OLIVE GARDEN TOASTED RAVIOLI 145

10. OLIVE GARDEN SPAGHETTI DELLE ROCCA 147

11. EL POLLO LOCO CHICKEN 149

12. CHI-CHI'S BAKED CHICKEN CHIMICHANGAS 151

13. OLIVE GARDEN'S SCALOPPINI ROMANA 153

14. OLIVE GARDEN STYLE SHRIMP CRISTOFORO 155

15. CPK BROCCOLI AND SUN-DRIED TOMATO FUSILLI 157

16. STOUFFER'S GRANDMA'S CHICKEN AND RICE BAKE 159

17. THE OLIVE GARDEN'S CAPELLINI PRIMAVERA 161

18. TGI FRIDAY'S BRUSCHETTA CHICKEN PASTA 163

19. OLIVE GARDEN POLLO LIMONE 167

20. MACCARONI GRILL'S SCALOPPINE DI POLLO 169

21. CLAIM JUMPER'S POT ROAST AND VEGETABLES 171

22. CHILI'S SPICY GARLIC-AND-LIME SHRIMP 173

23. OLIVE GARDEN'S RISOTTO MILANESE 175

24. DAVE AND BUSTER'S BLACKENED CHICKEN PASTA 177

CHAPTER 11: OTHER SIDES AND SAUCES RECIPES 179

1. BOSTON MARKET CORNBREAD 179

2. HOUSTON'S SPINACH AND ARTICHOKE DIP 181

3. FAMOUS DAVE'S BARBECUE SAUCE 183

4. STEAK & ALE'S BURGUNDY MUSHROOMS 185

5. GOLDEN CORRAL'S ROLLS 187

6. DER WEINER SCHNITZEL'S CHILI SAUCE 189

7. OLIVE GARDEN'S SAN REMO SEAFOOD DIP 191

8. DAVE AND BUSTER'S CHEDDAR MASHED POTATOES 193

9. OLIVE GARDEN'S GNOCCHI WITH SPICY TOMATO AND WINE SAUCE 195

10. LAWRY'S CREAMED SPINACH 197

11. OLIVE GARDEN'S ITALIAN SAUSAGE–STUFFED PORTOBELLO MUSHROOMS WITH AN HERB AND PARMESAN CHEESE 199

CHAPTER 12: DESSERT RECIPES 201

1. SUBWAY WHITE CHOCOLATE MACADAMIA NUT COOKIES 201

2. OLIVE GARDEN APPLE CARMELINA 203

3. GOLDEN CORRAL BREAD PUDDING 205

4. CRACKER BARREL CHERRY CHOCOLATE COBBLER 207

5. OLIVE GARDEN'S GOLDEN CINNAMON ORZO CALABRESE 209

6. APPLEBEE'S BLONDIE BROWNIES 211

7. APPLEBEE'S STRAWBERRY DESSERT SHOOTERS 213

8. CHEESECAKE FACTORY OREO CHEESECAKE 215

9. ARBY'S APPLE TURNOVERS 217

.... 218

10. HOSTESS SNOWBALLS 219

11. OLIVE GARDEN APPLE CARMELINA 221

12. BENNIGAN'S DEATH BY CHOCOLATE CAKE 223

13. PIZZA HUT DESSERT PIZZA 225

14. BOB EVANS PEANUT BUTTER PIE 227

15. STARBUCKS BLACK BOTTOM CUPCAKES 229

16. CHEESECAKE FACTORY PUMPKIN CHEESECAKE 231

17. THE MELTING POT FLAMING TURTLE FONDUE 233

18. TACO BELL CARAMEL APPLE EMPANADAS 235

19. CHILI'S MIGHTY ICE CREAM PIE 237

20. JUST-LIKE ENTENMANN'S RASPBERRY CHEESE DANISH 239

21. STARBUCKS OATMEAL COOKIES 241

22. CHILI'S MOLTEN LAVA CAKE 243

23. CRACKER BARREL CARROT CAKE 245

24. CRACKER BARREL BANANA PUDDING 247

25. WALDORF ASTORIA RED VELVET CAKE 249

26. OLIVE GARDEN STRAWBERRIES ROMANO 251

.... 252

27. CHILI'S CHOCOLATE CHIP PARADISE PIE 253

28. OUTBACK STEAKHOUSE KEY LIME PIE 255

29. THE MELTING POT DARK CHOCOLATE RASPBERRY FONDUE 257

30. APPLEBEE'S CHOCOLATE SIN CAKE 259

CHAPTER 13: BEVERAGES RECIPES..**261**

    1. Galiano 261

    2. Olive Garden Sangria 263

    3. Orange Julius.. 265

    4. Harry's Bar Bellini 267

    5. Applebee's Banana Berry Freeze 269

    6. Bennigan's Candy Bar Drink 273

    7. Chili's Calypso Cooler 275

    8. Chili's Electric Lemonade 277

    9. Outback Steakhouse Wallaby Darned.................................. 279

    10. T.G.I. Friday's Chocolate Monkey 281

    11. T.G.I. Friday's Flying Grasshopper 283

    12. Tommy Bahama Millionaire Mojito 285

CONCLUSION **287**

Introduction

People regularly tend to go out for dining at their favorite restaurants, but the stats reveal that the financial issues and economic constraints act as an obstacle, and hence people are compelled to spend less and remain unsatisfied.

If you are one of those people, why not opt for cooking copycat recipes at your home for the whole of your family?

In this book, you will learn how to cook those expensive and exquisite delicacies at home in your kitchen with the materials and products easily available at the market and grocery stores without spending any extra penny.

You will find step-by-step directions to cook the recipes, and you will be confident that the food you have in restaurants is served in hygienic conditions because you're going to prepare it yourself.

You don't need to be a Michelin chef to cook these recipes; even a rookie can easily turn the raw materials into amazing restaurant dishes.

In this book, you will find simple tips on how to create a restaurant feeling at home. A list of basic cookware and appliances that you need to have in your kitchen are also provided in this book.

Also, the basic cooking terms and techniques used by the restauranters are provided in this book.

Another benefit of this Recipes Cookbook is that one can alter dishes as per taste and dietary guidelines.

Restaurant foods contain more fat, salt, and sugar than we should have in our diets, and hence this book provides you with the freedom to change the recipe as per your likings. You can use these recipes and substitute the food items for a low-calorie meal.

Cooking the copycat recipes also gives you the freedom to control the portion size and, in a way, controls the wastage of food.

Also, you are not time-bound to finish the three-course meal. While cooking at home, you can take a break from the meal and have dessert and coffee several hours later, which you cannot do in a restaurant.

By cooking the restaurant copycat recipes at home, you will prepare dishes from several different restaurants in one sitting and can enjoy it all in the comfort of your home.

Chapter 1: How to Create the Feeling of a Restaurant at Home

Approximately three days a week, most families eat out. You know, whether you have a large family or even a small family of big eaters, you know that the expense easily adds up. It might be a smart choice to have a less expensive alternative to eating out when inflation rises in all aspects of the market. Your family would greatly admire the commitment you make to prepare daily meals with a restaurant-quality recipe.

The meal cooked at the restaurants take a lot of years to perfect in most situations, but you can have them, tried and true, to feed your family piping hot.

Wherever the expectations are, selecting the ingredients is no longer difficult in most restaurant recipes.

With a little detective work and a brief stay to the nearest grocery store, you can deliver a dinner that no one will be able to resist. You will be shocked at the savings you will accumulate when you use a copycat restaurant recipe instead of dining out.

If you are planning a meal, you can make a copycat restaurant recipe, which will have your guests saying that you have bought it from the restaurant that made the dish famous.

You can love the praise your cooking will offer while preparing to build a copycat restaurant meal for your next party or brunch or dinner.

Only because you're preparing your food doesn't mean it can't be as delicious as a five-star restaurant; a few easy tools are all you need. You don't need to be a master chef, either, to cook like one.

In this book, the equipment used to prepare the recipes is categorized into appliances, cooking gadgets, cookware, and bakeware. To make a great restaurant-quality dinner, you will also learn the terminology and techniques required.

Chapter 2: Cooking Tools Needed

Appliances

In your kitchen, the following appliances would have the greatest convenience and versatility:

- Electric mixer

- Blender

- Deep

- George Foreman Indoor Grill

- Microwave oven

Cooking Gadgets

A good cook acknowledges that a good-quality knife set will do more than any mechanical gadget in the kitchen. It would be best if you had at least the following knives in your kitchen.

- A chef's knife

- A bread knife

- A paring

To make your cooking experience more fun, there are a few simple safety guidelines you can follow:

1. The place to go barefoot is not the kitchen;

2. Understanding your instruments and how to treat them properly is crucial.

3. Learn the instructions for how the appliances should be used.

Other Tools

Other instruments used in the preparation of food include:

- Bottle opener

- Rolling pin

- Can opener

- Cutting board

- Set of mixing bowls

- Grater

- Meat mallet

- Colander

- Pizza cutter

- Set of measuring cups

- Long-handled forks, spoons, and spatulas

- Set of measuring spoons

Cookware

You'll need the following cookware items as well:

- 12″ nonstick skillets

- Saucepans with lids (small, medium, and large)

- Cast-iron skillet (for use in the oven)

- Stockpot

- Bakeware

Don't forget these necessary pieces of bakeware:

- Baking sheets Casserole dishes (small, medium, and large)

- Rectangular sheet cake pan

- Muffin pan

- Roasting pan with a rack

- Pizza pan

- Stocking the Pantry

Chapter 3: Basic Ingredients Required

Here is a list of essential items that your pantry should have. You should customize things on the list, of course, to fit the likes and dislikes of your family.

Herbs and Spices

Some of the most common and widely used flavors are:

- Barbecue seasoning
- Cajun seasoning
- Italian seasoning
- Lemon pepper seasoning
- Mexican seasoning

Sauces

- Barbecue sauce

- Olive oil

- Soups in a can

- Wine (red and white suitable, for drinking)

- Packages of dried onion soup mix

- Hot pepper sauce

- Packages of salad dressing mix

- Soy sauce

- Chili sauce

- Sweet and sour sauce

- Teriyaki sauce

- Steak sauce

- Vinegar (red, rice, and balsamic)

- Worcestershire sauce

Basic Grocery Items

These kitchen basics include:

- Beans (a variety of canned and dried)

- Rice (white, long-grain, wild, brown)

- Tomato sauce

- Bouillon cubes and powders

- Crackers (a variety)

- Meats (canned tuna, chicken, crab, and clams)

- Pasta (a mixed variety)

- Olives (black and green)

- Salsa

- Croutons

- Tomatoes (a variety of canned)

- Cooking oil

- Tomato paste

- Bread crumbs

Baking Items

You need to keep some basic baking ingredients in your pantry to bake like the finest restaurants, including:

- Baking mix

- Yeast

- Baking powder

- Baking soda

- Vegetable shortening

- Brown sugar

- Sweetened condensed milk

- Confectioners' sugar

- Sugar

- Honey

- Cocoa powder

- Pancake mix

- Cornstarch

- Flavored chips (chocolate, peanut butter, caramel)

- Nuts (a variety)

- Flour

For Desserts

You should have the following on hand to make more restaurant-inspired desserts:

- Applesauce

- Fixings for ice cream sundaes

- Canned fruits

- Puddings

- Cake mixes, brownies, and frostings

Chapter 4: Stored Ingredients

In the Refrigerator

Keep these things in the fridge handy to cook up your copycat recipes without the supermarket running out. Please make sure to have:

- Butter or margarine

- Cream

- Ketchup

- Mayonnaise

- Salad dressings

- Milk

- Salad fixings (a variety of fresh vegetables)

- Eggs

- Cheeses (a good variety)

- Sour cream

- Mustard

In the Freezer

There are a few things that you would still want to have stocked in your fridge, even if you won't need them every day.

Included are:

- Baguettes
- Vegetables (broccoli, spinach, sliced green peppers)
- Ground beef
- Boneless, skinless chicken breasts
- Steaks
- Bread and pizza dough
- Stew meat

Chapter 5: How to Choose Best Ingredients

It tastes easier to cook from scratch. The chefs of the restaurant look for the freshest foods they can find, and so do you. Whenever you can, avoid prepackaged products.

Whenever you can, avoid prepackaged products. Similar brands can deliver a cheaper price, but check the consistency and flavor, and the final taste of the dish may not please you.

You can transform an average meal into something special by upgrading your choices. Try romaine or a spring mix, for example, instead of using plain iceberg lettuce, and do not settle for dull American cheese.

Experiment with different flavors and try them.

Chicken

A whole chicken or any number of pre-cut packets may be bought. To prevent cross-contamination and salmonella risk, the trick to cooking with chicken is to be cautious. Before cooking, wash your hands and the chicken. On the kitchen table, keep the uncooked chicken separate from everything else, and use a different cutting board and knife just for the uncooked chicken, and don't use anything else for the same utensils. Thoroughly scrub anything the chicken touches. Cooking with chicken is perfectly safe if you follow these precautions.

Meats

A rosy bloom should be on red meats, and poultry should look plump and moist. Meat packets should be wrapped securely, without any leaks or extra moisture. To guarantee that the meat is fresh and processed appropriately, verify expiration dates and product branding. Refrigerate the beef as soon as you buy it. Price is not necessarily a quality reflection; never believe that the best is the most expensive meat.

Beef

According to the USDA, ground beef should not contain more than 30 percent fat by weight, so all the packets can mention their fat content. Get to know your butcher, and make him grind it up for you to get quality ground beef at a steep discount.

When selecting a steak, the items to look for are the grade and the cut. The grade refers to the age of the animal and the meat marble.

The best steaks are rated by the USDA as prime, followed by preference and variety. Often, look at the marbling or stripes of fat flowing across the beef when picking a steak. You want thin streaks that offer the perfect taste.

The rib provides rib roast, back ribs, and rib-eye steaks.

The short loin produces the tastiest steaks, such as the T-bone, Porterhouse, New York Strip, and the greatest cut tenderloin. Cuts of steak are taken from multiple parts of the animal. Often thaw meat for optimum protection in the refrigerator.

Also, on packets of raw meat, check for the healthy handling tag. It will instruct you how to stock, treat, and healthily cook meat and poultry.

Pork

The USDA inspects all pork found in grocery outlets. Look for cuts with a very limited amount of fat on the outside and meat that is strong and grayish pink in color when purchasing pork.

The meat should have a limited amount of jelly for a better taste. Four fundamental cuts distinguish all the other cuts: the leg, the side, the loin, and the shoulder. You'll get bacon, ground pork for sausage rolls, ribs, roasts, chops, and ham from those cuts.

Fish

Knowing how to pick fresh fish is a talent that any cook needs to have. The scent of fresh fish needs to be like pure water. The fish's eyes should be white and translucent, and the gills should be a bright, rich red color. Do not buy it if it feels unpleasant or looks discolored.

Vegetables

Before you buy, take the time to check each vegetable. Look for vegetables that are crisp, plump, and brightly colored. Ignore the shriveled, bruised, moldy, or blemished ones.

Asparagus, with closed ends having straight stalks that are compact, are best to be bought.

The best to pick are beans that are brightly colored and crisp.

It is best to avoid broccoli heads that are light green and yellowish.

Without brown spots, cabbage should have bright leaves. Cauliflower should not be preferred with withered leaves and brown spots.

The stalks of celery should have firm, crisp ribs.

Cucumbers should not have soft spots and should be firm.

It is worth avoiding peas that are wilted or have brown stains.

It is important to pick peppers that are crisp and brightly colored.

The leaves of spinach should be crisp and moisture-free.

Take the opportunity to talk at the store with the people in the produce department. When the trucks come to the store, they will tell you to recognize when the freshest items are placed on the shelf.

Fruits

When picking your fruit, look for tenderness, plumpness, and bright color. Fruits should be heavy and clear from scratches, wounds, mildew, mold, or any other blemishes for their scale. At either point of ripeness, bananas are sold and should be kept at room temperature.

Berries can quickly break from their roots. Keep them refrigerated

It is appropriate to select melons that have a sweet aromatic fragrance. A heavy odor means they are overripe.

When they are ripe, oranges, grapefruits, and lemons are sold. For 2–3 weeks, you can store them in the refrigerator.

Chapter 6: Cooking Terms and Techniques That are must Know

In the kitchen, performance comes with a knowledge of cooking vocabulary, and the secret to cooking a successful restaurant-quality meal is proper technique.

Before being used in a recipe, most ingredients are chopped into smaller pieces. Often, in shape and size, you like standardized pieces; other times, it doesn't matter. Here are the basic methods for cutting.

Cutting Methods

- **Chopping** corresponds to just breaking into smaller bits. It's a bigger cut, and it doesn't have to be standardized than dice or mince. To chop vegetables, hold the tip of the chef's knife on the cutting board and, with a rocking action, cut evenly down into the vegetable. Bring the object that is chopped into the blade, holding the fingers firmly curled.

- **Mincing** is a cut of food that is very thin. To mince, loosely slice it on a cutting board. Gather the pieces together in a pile. Place your knife above the stack. Shift the blade in an arc, holding the tip meets the cutting surface, repeatedly raising and lowering the blade's length down to anything you are mincing.

- **Dicing** is a cube that typically has a square of 1/4"-3/4". Break it into panels of the thickness you like your dice. Stack the panels and cut the distance that you like the dice to be uniform matchsticks. Then line up and cut the sticks into a dice.

- **Julienne** involves cutting through long strips of something. Normally, this is achieved for vegetables.

- **Slicing** is where an item such as beef, fruit, vegetables, cheese, or bread is completely sliced into

- **Grating** provides a very good texture to food, which can be achieved using a portable grater or box grater.

- **Zesting** is the method of extracting a citrus fruit peel's outer part.

- Maintenance of the knife is a required skill because a sharp knife is a secure knife. It is an indispensable kitchen tool that must be carefully handled to keep it in full working order. Take the time to sharpen your knives; otherwise, you can trip and allow yourself to be sliced by a dull knife. Different techniques are available to prepare meat and vegetables for cooking.

Other Basic Concepts that are must know

The following terms and concepts should be known by the person cooking like a restaurant chef. They are briefly stated as under:

1. In Italian, 'al dente' means 'to the tooth' and is a term for pasta that suggests that it is cooked only to preserve a strong texture.
2. Basting is to moisten the food with pan drippings or a sauce during cooking to avoid drying and add flavor.
3. Blanching consists of frying food partially in boiling water.
4. For rough meat cuts, braising is the preferred cooking process, where they are cooked slowly in a limited amount of liquid.
5. Brining is a method of soaking food in salted water.
6. Broil refers to cooking food under direct fire.
7. A butterfly is to break food down the middle without dividing the halves entirely.
8. Deep fry is to cook food in ample hot oil to cover the food until it is crispy.
9. Marinate means standing food in a liquid to intensify and tenderize the taste.

10. Poaching means preparing a meal by submerging it in a liquid that is simmering.

11. Roasting is a process used in an oven to prepare food.

12. Searing requires browning meat to lock in the juices easily on elevated heat.

13. Simmer means preparing a liquid food that is kept only below the point of boiling.

14. Sauté is a limited quantity of cooking oil for cooking or browning beef.

15. Steaming is the method of cooking food by boiling water in the vapor given off.

16. Stew means boiling food in liquid for a long time, before soft, in a closed oven.

17. Stir-frying is an Asian practice of cooking small pieces in hot oil quickly while continuously stirring.

Food Presentation

The vibes around the spot become as critical as the food's nature served in deciding whether or not you have a satisfying experience if you go to an amazing restaurant. Note that when preparing a copycat meal in a restaurant, food presentation and table decor is of paramount importance.

Garnishes

As for garnishes, the ingredients in the dish may do double duty. Just before plating, save some fresh chopped herbs needed in the dish to add. On top of a platter, use sliced tomatoes or green onions. In almost every dish, shredded or shaved cheeses add a good touch.

Plating

Restaurants use many kinds of plating methods, including:

1. The pie style is where the plate is broken with a protein, starch, and vegetable portion.
2. The half-and-half type of plating is where the main dish, with the accompaniments located on the other, is on one side of the plate.
3. Vertical plating is where, usually with the protein on the bottom and the side dishes on top, you build the plate upwards.
4. Plating in the family-style is where the food is served on large platters expected to be shared.

Presenting Desserts

Serve them in individual glass drinking glasses to display your wonderfully made restaurant desserts. A good presentation is made from a small wine glass layered with cake and ice cream or fruit and yogurt.

In restaurants, dessert shots are all the rage right now. Small sweet desserts are a sensation all over America that has made its way into dessert carts.

Small mini parfaits, sundaes, and layered desserts in shot glasses may be quickly modified for the home chef. It is time to raid your bar and fill the dessert with those shot glasses. Small juice glasses containing small-sized after-dinner snacks also fit well.

Chapter 7: Appetizer Recipes

1. Olive Garden's Clam Bruschetta

Preparation time: In about 35 minutes
Servings: 4
Difficulty: Moderate

Ingredients:

- Eight thick diagonally cut slices of Italian or French bread
- One clove garlic, cut in half
- Four large tomatoes, cut into eight thick slices
- One cup of chopped canned clam meat, drained
- Kosher salt
- Black pepper
- Half cup extra virgin olive oil
- 12 fresh basil leaves, shredded

Instructions:

1. Preheat the broiler or grill.

2. From both sides, toast the slices of bread. Rub the garlic with the split side of it.

3. On each slice of toasted bread, place one tomato slice and two tablespoons of clam meat and arrange the slices on a warmed serving tray. Sprinkle with salt and a few black pepper bits.

4. Sprinkle with olive oil and apply fresh basil to the top. Serve it warm.

2. Girl Scout Samoa Cookies

Preparation time: In about 35 minutes

Servings: 1

Difficulty: Moderate

Ingredients:

- Six tablespoons butter

- Half cup of sugar

- Half cup of light corn syrup

- Half of 14–oz can sweeten condensed milk

- Half teaspoon of vanilla

- Four cups of toasted coconut

- One cup of semi–sweet or milk chocolate chips

Instructions:

1. Combine the butter, sugar and corn syrup in a 2-quart saucepan over medium-low heat. Heat to a full boil, stirring with a wooden spoon constantly. Boil for 3 minutes, continuously stirring.

2. Pour in the sweetened condensed milk gently, stirring continuously. Continue to cook until the candy thermometer hits 220-228 degrees F over low heat.

3. Withdraw from the heat. Stir the vanilla in. Beat yourself until creamy. Stir in the toasted coconut instantly and combine properly.

4. Heap tablespoons of spoon mixture into spherical mounds on buttered waxed parchment. Slightly flatten and stab a small round hole into the middle of each cookie with the end of a wooden spoon. Let it cool.

5. Melt the chocolate chips and thinly drizzle over the cookies in strips to allow the chocolate to harden at room temperature. Store in an airtight container.

3. Olive Garden's Bruschetta

Preparation time: In about 30 minutes

Servings: 2 to 4

Difficulty: Moderate

Ingredients:

- Three firm Roma tomatoes, finely diced (about One and a Half C.)
- One tablespoon of minced fresh basil
- Two teaspoons of minced garlic
- One teaspoon of extra virgin olive oil
- One teaspoon of balsamic vinegar
- A quarter teaspoon of salt
- 9-10 slices of ciabatta bread (or Italian bread)
- One tablespoon of grated Parmesan cheese
- pinch dried parsley flakes

Instructions:

1. In a medium bowl, toss the diced tomatoes with basil, garlic, olive oil, vinegar, and salt.
2. For 1 hour, cover and chill. Pre-heat the oven to 450F until you are about to serve the dish.
3. In a shallow bowl, mix the parmesan cheese with the dried parsley. On a baking sheet, arrange the bread slices.
4. On each bread slice, sprinkle a few pinches of the parmesan cheese mixture.
5. Bake for 5 minutes or until the bread becomes crispy.
6. Add the tomato mixture to a baking dish and eat with the slices of toasted bread.

4. Famous Dave's Dragon Firecracker Chicken Wings

Preparation time: In about 50 minutes

Servings: 4

Difficulty: Moderate

Ingredients:

Wing Dust

- Two tablespoons of anise seeds
- Two tablespoons of salt
- Two tablespoons of Chinese five-spice powder
- Three tablespoons of superfine sugar
- One tablespoon of paprika

- One tablespoon of garlic seasoning

- Two teaspoons of cayenne pepper

- Two teaspoons of black pepper

- One teaspoon of garlic powder

Wings

- 24 chicken wings

- Two cups of the chicken marinade, homemade or store-bought

- Peanut oil for frying

- All-purpose flour for coating the wings

- Eight tablespoons of (1 stick) butter, melted

- Famous Dave's Devil's Spit hot sauce

- Sweet-and-sour sauce, for serving

Instructions:

1. Make Famous Dave's Dragon Wing Dust first. For that, in a spice grinder, grind the anise seeds to a fine powder. Combine and grind with the remaining dust elements. Store in a container with a lid.

2. In the fridge, marinate the wings in the marinade of your choosing for 4 hours. Drain the wings of the marinade and dispose of it. Heat 3/4 inch of peanut oil up to 375 degrees F. Toss in the flour with the wings; shake off the surplus.

3. Fry the wings until they are golden brown and cooked through, working in batches. Move to a tray for baking.

4. Combine the hot sauce and molten butter. Cover each of the wings with a pastry brush, then sprinkle generously with the Dragon Wing Dust. Use sweet-and-sour sauce to serve.

5. Outback-Style Sweet Potato

Preparation time: In about 35 minutes

Servings: 1

Difficulty: Easy

Ingredients:

- One large sweet potato

- Two tablespoons of shortening

- Two to Three tablespoons of kosher salt

- Three tablespoons of softened butter

- Three tablespoons of honey

- One teaspoon of cinnamon

Instructions:

1. Rub with the shortening outside of the potato and dust with kosher salt. Bake the potatoes for 45 to 60 minutes, at 350 degrees F (until soft).

2. Then slice the potato. Whip the butter and honey together and place them inside.

3. Sprinkle with cinnamon and then serve.

6. Olive Garden Style Tortellini Do Forni

Preparation time: In about 40 minutes

Servings: 4

Difficulty: Moderate

Ingredients:

- One and A quarter lbs. cheese tortellini, cooked

- fresh parsley, chopped

- fresh Parmesan, grated

- Tomato basil cream sauce

- A quarter C. olive oil

- Two large cloves of garlic, minced

- Two C. plum tomatoes; peeled, crushed, drained

- One chicken bouillon cubed, mashed

- Four teaspoons of dried basil

- Two teaspoons of fresh parsley, chopped

- A quarter teaspoon of black pepper

- Two C. heavy cream

- Four tablespoons of fresh Parmesan, grated

Instructions:

1. Slice the tomatoes into large chunks. Blend the basil, parsley and pepper bouillon into the tomatoes.

2. In olive oil, sauté the garlic and bring it to a simmer. Add the milk to a non-aluminum skillet and bring it to a slow boil until the sauce is hot, then add the hot tomato sauce and cheese.

3. Stir well, then combine the tortellini in the tomato basil cream saucepan.

4. Serve top with cheese and parsley.

7. Pepperidge Farm Sausalito Cookies

Preparation time: In about 45 minutes

Servings: 2 to 4

Difficulty: Moderate

Ingredients:

- One pound of butter softened
- Two eggs
- Two teaspoons vanilla
- One and a half cup of granulated sugar
- One and a half cups brown sugar
- One teaspoon baking powder
- One and a half teaspoons baking soda
- One teaspoon salt
- Five cups of flour
- One and a half 12 oz. Packages semi-sweet choc. chips
- Three cups of chopped macadamia nuts

Instructions:

1. In a bowl, combine the creamy butter, eggs, and vanilla.
2. Sift together the sugar, baking powder, baking soda, salt, and flour in another bowl.
3. Combine the egg/butter mixture with the dry mixture. Add the nuts and chocolate chips.
4. Form into 1-inch balls, and put on an unbuttered baking sheet 1 inch apart.
5. Bake for 10 to 11 minutes at 375F.

8. Famous Amos Chocolate Chip Cookies

Preparation time: In about 45 minutes

Servings: 1

Difficulty: Moderate

Ingredients:

- ¼ cup shortening
- ¼ cup butter, softened (half a stick)
- Half cup of brown sugar
- A quarter cup granulated sugar

- One egg

- One teaspoon of vanilla extract

- Two tablespoons of milk

- Two cups of all-purpose flour

- ¾ teaspoon of baking soda

- Half teaspoon of salt

- One cup of mini semisweet chocolate chips

Instructions:

1. The oven should be preheated to 350 degrees F. Line parchment paper or baking mats with cookie sheets.

2. In an electric blender fitted with a paddle extension, build butter, shortening, and sugars together. Whisk together the potato, vanilla, and milk. Sprinkle with salt and baking soda.

3. Stir in the flour and blend until mixed. Stir the chocolate chips together.

4. Scoop up one tablespoon of dough balls and put them on cookie sheets. With the palm of your hand, press the dough gently to flatten just a little (about half the thickness of the ball).

5. Bake until the cookies are finely browned, for around 13 minutes.

6. Remove from oven, cool 5 minutes on cookie sheet before removing to rack to cool completely.

9. Boston Market Dill Potato Wedges

Preparation time: In about 40-50 minutes

Servings: 4 to 6

Difficulty: Moderate

Ingredients:

- Seven or Eight new red potatoes

- Two cloves' garlic, minced fine

- A quarter-pound of butter

- Half teaspoon of salt

- Half teaspoon of black pepper

- Half teaspoon of celery salt

- Two teaspoons of dried dill weed

Instructions:

1. Wash the potatoes well and boil them until they're barely tender. Drain the potatoes and cut them into wedges.

2. In a large frying pan, melt one butter stick (use only real butter) and sauté the garlic for about one minute.

3. Stir in the potatoes and the remaining seasonings.

4. Pan-fry the potatoes until finely browned.

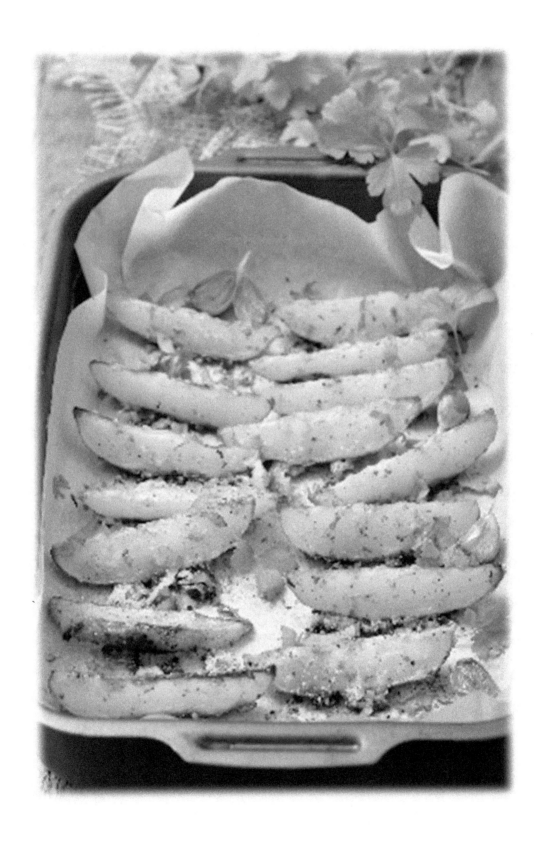

10. Chili's Boneless Buffalo Wings

Preparation time: In about 35 minutes

Servings: 2 to 4

Difficulty: Moderate

Ingredients:

- One cup of all-purpose flour
- Two teaspoons of salt
- Half teaspoon black pepper
- 1⁄4 teaspoon cayenne pepper
- 1⁄4 teaspoon paprika

- One egg, beaten

- One cup of milk

- Two boneless, skinless chicken breasts, each sliced into six pieces

- Four to six cups of vegetable oil

- One tablespoon of butter or margarine

- 1/4 cup Crystal or Frank's hot sauce

For Serving

- Celery sticks

- Blue cheese dressing, homemade or store-bought

Instructions:

1. Combine the flour and dry seasonings in a medium bowl and whisk until well mixed. Whisk the egg and the milk together individually.

2. In the egg mixture, dip each chicken piece, shake it a little, then dip it in the flour mixture. On a baking sheet, lay the bits and refrigerate for 15 minutes.

3. Heat four cups of vegetable oil to 375 ° F in a large skillet. To fry the chicken, keep extra oil handy in case you need more.

4. Melt the butter and add the hot sauce; place it in a big bowl to set aside.

5. Fry the chicken pieces in batches until golden brown and fried (no longer pink in the middle). Drain on towels made of cloth. Place it in the butter-hot sauce mixture when all the chicken is fried, and toss.

6. Serve it on the side with celery sticks and blue cheese dressing.

11. Olive Gardens Fried Mozzarella

Preparation time: In about 40 minutes

Servings: 2 to 4

Difficulty: Moderate

Ingredients:

- One pound block of mozzarella cheese
- Two eggs, beaten
- A quarter cup of water
- One and a half cups of Italian bread crumbs
- Half teaspoon granulated garlic
- Half teaspoon dried oregano
- Half teaspoon dried basil
- 2/3 cup flour
- 1/3 cup corn starch

Instructions:

1. Split the cheese block into half-inch pieces lengthwise. Break each component in half.
2. With water, beat the eggs and set them aside. Mix and set aside the bread crumbs, garlic, oregano and basil.
3. Blend the flour with the starch from the corn and set aside.
4. Heat the vegetable oil to 350F for deep frying.
5. Dip the cheese in the flour, wash the eggs, and cover with the bread crumbs.
6. Place in the hot oil carefully and fry until golden brown.
7. Drain in brown paper bags and eat with the warmed pasta sauce you want.

12. Bennigan's Broccoli Bites

Preparation time: In about 40 minutes

Servings: 4

Difficulty: Easy

Ingredients:

Broccoli Bites

- Two cups of frozen chopped broccoli
- Three eggs
- 3/4 cup shredded Colby cheese
- 3/4 cup shredded Monterey jack cheese
- Five tablespoons of real bacon bits

- One tablespoon of diced yellow onion
- Two tablespoons of flour
- Four cups of oil for frying
- Italian breadcrumbs, as needed

Honey-Mustard Dipping Sauce

- 3⁄4 cup sour cream
- 1/3 cup mayonnaise
- 1/3 cup Dijon mustard
- 1/3 cup honey
- Four teaspoons of lemon juice

Instructions:

1. Thaw and properly drain the broccoli by squeezing it into a strainer. Using a whisk to beat the eggs in a mixing bowl until well mixed.

2. In a plastic container, put the broccoli, eggs, cheese, bacon bits, onion, and flour. Stir together until completely mixed with a spatula.

3. Refrigerate the mixture for 1 hour or so. This will aid in binding the blend, making preparing even easier.

4. In a fryer or deep pan, heat about 4 cups of oil at 350 °F. In a shallow pan, put the bread crumbs. Scoop in the bread crumbs for one tablespoon of a part of the broccoli mixture. Shape each part into a ball and cover it in the bread crumbs well.

5. Place the bites of broccoli in the frying basket or frying pan. Let aware they're not going to stay together. Fry for a minute.

6. Remove and place the excess oil on a plate lined with paper towels to absorb it.

7. Combine the sour cream, mayonnaise and mustard for the dipping sauce. Using a whisk, mix thoroughly. Pour the honey and lemon juice in slowly and blend until it is smooth and well mixed.

8. Serve with broccoli bites.

13. Red Lobster's Ultimate Fondue

Preparation time: In about 40 minutes

Servings: 4

Difficulty: Moderate

Ingredients:

- One cup of Velveeta, cubed

- One cup of swiss cheese in small pieces

- One can Campbell's condensed cream of shrimp soup

- One cup of milk

- Half teaspoon of cayenne

- Half teaspoon of paprika

- One broiled lobster tail (or one and a half cups of imitation) – chopped

Instructions:

1. In a medium saucepan, mix all but the lobster and cook over low heat until melted, sometimes stirring.

2. Stir in the lobster meat until it's melted.

3. Garnish, if needed, with diced red pepper and serve with French bread.

14. Morton's Steakhouse Shrimp Alexander

Preparation time: In about 35 minutes

Servings: 4

Difficulty: Moderate

Ingredients:

Breaded Shrimp

- Four ounces melted butter
- One pound of jumbo shrimp (8-12) to the pound
- One cup of plain breadcrumbs
- Three teaspoons of finely minced shallots
- Two teaspoons of finely chopped parsley

- One and a half tablespoons of finely chopped fresh garlic
- salt and pepper to taste

Beurre Blanc Sauce

- Three tablespoons of finely minced shallots
- Half cup of dry white wine inexpensive chardonnay is fine
- One to Two tablespoons of lemon juice
- Eight ounces unsalted butter
- A quarter teaspoon of salt

Instructions:

For Shrimp

1. Preheat the oven to 500 F.

2. Put the breadcrumbs, shallots, parsley and garlic together. To taste, you might want to add some salt and pepper.

3. Shell, devein and butterfly the shrimp

4. Dip the shrimp in butter (butter should be soft, not hot), then in a mixture of breadcrumbs, put the shrimp on the side of a small pan. Pour the excess butter into the pan so that the butter will cook the shrimp.

Beurre Blanc

5. In a shallow pan, mix the champagne, lemon juice, and shallots. Heat over moderate flame.

6. Reduce the heat to the lowest setting on your burner until the wine has decreased to just a tablespoon. Start applying butter to the small nobs, constantly stirring until the butter melts.

7. Continuously stir the sauce, adding more butter just after the last addition has melted and thickened the sauce.

8. When the sauce has thickened and is pale yellow, the sauce is full. Do not allow it to get too hot for the sauce, or it will split.

15. Red Lobster's Shrimp Diablo

Preparation time: In about 55 minutes

Servings: 4 to 6

Difficulty: Moderate

Ingredients:

- Three lb. Large Uncooked Shrimp in the Shells (no heads)
- Milk
- Half lb. Unsalted Butter
- One Jar Kraft BBQ Sauce
- Half cup of Ketchup
- One tablespoon of Fresh Ground Pepper
- A quarter cup of Frank's Red Hot-Sauce

Instructions:

1. Wash the shrimp in cool water, removing the heads if necessary.

2. Soak the shrimp overnight in milk.

3. In a saucepan, mix all the sauce ingredients and stir before ready to boil.

4. Remove from the heat and cool for four hours.

5. Drain the milk from the shrimp, put it in a baking dish and cover the sauce equally. Let it stand for 1 hour.

6. Bake in a preheated oven (450F) for 15 minutes, uncovered (less time for smaller shrimp).

16. Emeril's New Orleans's Rosemary Biscuits

Preparation time: In about 25 minutes

Servings: 12 biscuits

Difficulty: Easy

Ingredients:

- One cup of all-purpose flour, plus extra for dusting

- One teaspoon of baking powder

- Half a teaspoon of salt

- 1/8 teaspoon baking soda

- Three tablespoons of cold unsalted butter, cut into small pieces

- One tablespoon of minced fresh rosemary or One teaspoon of dried

- Half to 3/4 cup buttermilk

Instructions:

1. Preheat the oven to 450°F.

2. Mix the dry ingredients in a large bowl and whisk to blend thoroughly. Using a cookie cutter or two dinner knives to slice through the butter until the mixture resembles coarse crumbs. Add the rosemary, which is minced.

3. Drop about half a cup of buttermilk and carefully stir until the dough is just combined with a wooden spoon. Do not overmix since this would make the biscuits stiff. Add a little more buttermilk if the dough appears too stiff. Shape it softly into a dough ball.

4. Flour a work surface like a cutting board and pat the dough ball out to a width of around 7 inches and a half-inch thick circle. Break the biscuits and put them on a baking sheet using a 1-inch diameter cookie cutter.

5. In between the biscuits, make sure to leave plenty of space.

6. Bake for 10 to 12 minutes, until the biscuits are lightly golden brown on the top and the sides. Serve it warm.

17. Hard Rock Café's Tupelo-style Chicken

Preparation time: In about 50 minutes

Servings: 6 to 8

Difficulty: Moderate

Ingredients:

- Honey-Mustard Dipping Sauce

- ¼ cup mayonnaise

- One and a half teaspoons of yellow mustard

- Two teaspoons of honey

- Pinch of paprika

- Apricot Dipping Sauce

- Two tablespoons of Grey Poupon Dijon mustard

- One tablespoon of apricot preserves

- Two tablespoons of honey

- One cup of crumbled cornflakes

- Two teaspoons of red pepper flakes

- One and a quarter teaspoons of cayenne pepper

- One teaspoon of cumin

- One teaspoon of salt

- Half teaspoon of paprika

- A quarter teaspoon onion powder

- Pinch of garlic powder

- Four to six cups of vegetable oil for deep-frying

- One cup of milk

- One large egg, beaten

- One cup of all-purpose flour

- One pound of boneless, skinless chicken breasts

Instructions:

1. Make the sauce of honey-mustard. Whisk all of the ingredients together. Set aside in a fridge sealed until ready to use.

2. Create the apricot sauce by whisking together all of the ingredients. Set aside or, when ready to use, refrigerate, sealed.

3. Combine the cornflakes with the red pepper flakes, cayenne, cumin, cinnamon, paprika, onion powder, and garlic powder to make the bread. Whisk until it is well combined with the ingredients. Set in a shallow dish.

4. In a deep-fryer or a heavy-bottomed saucepan, preheat the oil to 350°F.

5. Whisk the milk and the egg together and put them in a shallow bowl. Put it in a shallow dish with the flour.

6. Split the chicken breasts into strips that are 1/2-inch wide. Cover in flour and the egg with each strip, then coat it again and coat the egg again. Press each strip into the cornflake mixture and fry it carefully, in lots, for 4 to 5 minutes before each strip is browned and fried through. Drain on towels made of cloth.

7. Serve with the two-hand ramekin dipping sauces.

Chapter 8: Soup Recipes

1. Applebee's French Onion Soup

Preparation time: In about 1 hour 20 minutes

Servings: 10 bowls

Difficulty: Hard

Ingredients:

- Three tablespoons of vegetable oil
- Six medium white onions, sliced
- Eight cups of good quality beef broth
- One cup of water

- Two and a half teaspoons salt
- Half teaspoon garlic powder
- A quarter teaspoon ground black pepper
- Five hamburger buns
- Ten slices of provolone cheese
- Ten teaspoons shredded parmesan cheese

Instructions:

1. Heat the vegetable oil over medium-high heat in a large soup pot or saucepan. Add the sliced onions and sauté until the onions appear to soften and become translucent for 20 minutes.

2. Bring the mixture of the beef broth, water, salt, garlic powder and black pepper in the pan. Reduce the heat and steam for 45 minutes until the soup starts to boil.

3. Separate the bottoms from the tops of the hamburger buns to create the croutons. Place the bottoms aside, then cut the tops' crown to give them the same size and shape as the bottoms.

4. Preheat the oven to 325F. Place the bread directly on the rack in the oven and bake for 15 to 20 minutes or until each slice is crispy and golden brown. And put aside.

5. Spoon around one cup into an oven-safe bowl until the soup is finished. On top of the broth, add a crouton, and add a slice of provolone cheese on top of the crouton. Sprinkle the Provolone with half a teaspoon of sliced parmesan cheese. Place the bowl in your high-broil oven unit.

6. Broil the soup or until the cheese is melted and begins to brown for 5 or 6 minutes.

7. Sprinkle over the top of the broth with an extra half teaspoon of melted parmesan cheese and eat. For the remaining cups, repeat.

2. Bennigan's Potato Soup

Preparation time: In about 1 hour

Servings: 4

Difficulty: Moderate

Ingredients:

- One and 3/4 oz. ham base
- Two quarts of chicken stock
- Eight oz. yellow onion, diced
- Three oz. margarine
- Two lbs. potatoes, bite-size
- One and a half teaspoons of Black pepper
- Two C. milk
- Three oz. flour
- Three oz. margarine

Instructions:

1. Combine the chicken stock with the base of the ham in a saucepan. Stir until the lumps dissolve.

2. Melt the first margarine measurement in a different stockpot; add onion and sauté until translucent. Add bite-sized potato parts and pepper. Add the mixture of chicken stock and whisk until well combined. Get it to a boil with the mixture.

3. Melt the second amount of margarine in a small pan and add flour to make a roux. They need to be light brown.

4. Add roux with a wire whisk as stock comes to a boil. This will cause the soup to begin to thicken.

5. Head to boil. Add the milk slowly. Create an extra roux if the soup is too thin and add it to the soup. If you need to do this, make sure that the roux is cooked until the color is tan. It would get rid of the flavor of raw flour. Thin it out with more milk if the soup is too thick.

3. Huston's Wild Rice and Mushroom Soup

Preparation time: In about 1 hour 30 minutes

Servings: 8 to 10

Difficulty: Hard

Ingredients:

- Two cups of wild rice

- Four tablespoons of (Half stick) butter

- One and 1/4 cups of finely diced carrots

- Four ounces leeks, finely diced

- One pound of mushrooms, sliced

- Half cup all-purpose flour

- Half cup of sherry

- One to two cups of vegetable broth

- Four cups of heavy cream

- Two tablespoons of chopped fresh thyme, or Two teaspoons of dried

- Three tablespoons of chopped fresh parsley, or One tablespoon of dried, plus extra for garnish

- Salt and pepper

Instructions:

1. Boil the wild rice in eight cups of water for 30 to 40 minutes until the grains appear to burst. Drain the rice and set aside or refrigerate until ready to use in a covered dish.

2. In a stockpot, warm the butter and gently sauté the carrots and leeks. Add the mushrooms when they are soft and cook until tender. Apply the flour to the pot and whisk it regularly until it is lightly brown and the butter is thoroughly incorporated.

3. Remove the vegetables from the pot, deglaze the sherry pot, scrape off any browned pieces, return the vegetables, and add the broth.

4. Simmer for 30 minutes, sometimes stirring. Add the heavy cream and the fried rice. Keep simmering until slightly thickened, then add the chopped herbs and season with salt and pepper to taste. If needed, ladle into warmed bowls to serve and garnish with extra parsley.

4. Olive Garden's Zuppa Toscana

Preparation time: In about 1 hour 50 minutes

Servings: 4

Difficulty: Hard

Ingredients:

- Half lb. hot Italian lean turkey sausage (2 large links)

- Three C. fat-free chicken broth

- Three C. fat-free milk

- One tablespoon of Hormel Real Bacon pieces

- A quarter teaspoon of salt

- dash of crushed red pepper flakes

- One medium russet potato

- Two C. chopped kale

Instructions:

1. Grill the sausage or sauté it until cooked. In a medium saucepan, add the chicken broth, cream, onion, bacon bits, salt, and pepper flakes over medium/high heat.

2. Lengthwise, quarter the potato, then carve into quarter-inch slices.

3. Add that to the saucepan. Reduce the heat and steam for 30 minutes until the mixture starts to boil.

4. Break the sausage into one-quarter-inch thick bits at an angle. To the saucepan, add the bacon.

5. Simmer for 1 hour or until the slices of the potato appear to soften. Attach the kale to the soup and steam for a further 10-15 minutes or until the potatoes are tender.

5. O' Charley's Baked Potato Soup

Preparation time: 50 minutes

Servings: 4

Difficulty: Moderate

Ingredients:

- Three lbs. red potatoes

- A quarter cup butter, melted

- A quarter cup flour

- Two quarts half–and–half

- One pound of block Velveeta cheese, melted

- White pepper, to taste

- Garlic powder, to taste

- One teaspoon of hot pepper sauce

- Half lb. bacon, fried crisply

- One cup of cheddar cheese, shredded

- Half cup of fresh chives, chopped

- Half cup of fresh parsley, chopped

Instructions:

1. Dice half-inch cubes of unpeeled red potatoes. Place it in a wide Dutch oven, cover it with water and bring it to a boil.

2. Let it simmer for 10 minutes or until nearly cooked.

3. Combine the melted margarine and flour in a separate, large Dutch oven, mixing until smooth. Place over low heat and add half and half steadily, continuously stirring.

4. Continue to stir until the mixture begins to thicken and smooth. Add Velveeta, melted. Stir well, Stir well.

5. Drain the potatoes and add the mixture to the sauce. Stir in the pepper, garlic powder and hot pepper sauce.

6. Cover and simmer for 30 minutes under low heat, stirring periodically.

7. Place the soup and finish with crumbled bacon, shredded cheese, chives and parsley in individual serving bowls.

6. Brennan's Onion Soup

Preparation time: In about 35 minutes

Servings: 8

Difficulty: Moderate

Ingredients:

- One and a half cups of butter
- Four cups of sliced onions
- One and 3/4 cups of all-purpose flour
- One to two cups of beef stock
- Half teaspoon Cayenne Pepper
- One and a half tablespoon salt
- One egg yolk
- Two tablespoons Cream

Instructions:

1. Melt butter in a six-quarter soup kettle, add onions, reduce the heat to very mild, and cook until the onions are melted.

2. In the first step of cooking, be careful not to tan. Add flour and simmer for an additional 5 to 10 minutes, stirring regularly. Combine with the stock, salt, and bring to a boil. Lower the flame and boil for 15 minutes or so.

3. Suspend the kettle from the heat. Whisk the egg yolk and milk together. Add a little broth and mix rapidly, and add to the kettle of soup.

4. Serve in soup cups with toasted bread or croutons and scatter with buttered breadcrumbs and grated Parmesan cheese.

5. Brown under the flaming broiler and serve.

7. Chili's Southwest Chicken Chili

Preparation time: In about 30 minutes

Servings: 4

Difficulty: Moderate

Ingredients:

- A quarter C. vegetable oil
- Half C. diced onions
- One and 1/3 C. diced green bell pepper
- Two tablespoons of diced seeded jalapeno pepper
- Three tablespoons of fresh minced garlic
- Four and a half C. water

- Eight teaspoons of chicken base
- Two teaspoons of lime juice
- Two tablespoons of granulated sugar
- Three tablespoons of cornstarch
- Three tablespoons of ground cumin
- Two and a half tablespoons of ground chili powder
- Four teaspoons of ground paprika
- Four teaspoons of dried basil
- Two teaspoons of freshly minced cilantro
- One and a half teaspoon of ground red pepper
- Half teaspoons of ground oregano
- Half C. crushed canned tomatillos
- One (4 oz.) can dice green chiles, drained
- Two (15 oz.) cans of navy beans or small white beans, drained
- One (15 oz.) can of dark red kidney beans, drained
- Three lb. diced cooked chicken breast
- Shredded cheese and sour cream for garnish (optional)
- Tortilla chips

Instructions:

1. In a 5 quart or bigger pot, heat oil over medium heat. Along with bell pepper, jalapeno and garlic, add onions and sauté.

2. Cook until you have tender vegetables. Combine the water, chicken base, lime juice, sugar, cornstarch and the seasonings in another container.

3. Add to the mixture of vegetables. In a saucepan, add tomatillos and diced green chilies; bring to a boil. Add the chicken and beans and cook for 10 minutes.

4. If desired, serve topped with cheese and sour cream on the side with tortilla chips.

8. Bob Evan's Cheddar Baked Potato Soup

Preparation time: In about 40 minutes

Servings: 4

Difficulty: Moderate

Ingredients:

- One can Campbell's Cheddar Cheese Soup

- One can of chicken broth

- One pound of grated Cheddar Cheese

- Four cups of whole milk

- One soup can

- Two tablespoons of butter

- Two tablespoons of Corn Starch

- Salt, Pepper, Onion powder and Garlic salt – Half teaspoon each

- Seven medium potatoes, diced to 1" and boiled

Instructions:

1. Add the soup, half the broth, half the milk, and stir.

2. Add milk and cheese. Add the cornstarch and the remainder of the broth to the soup.

3. Add butter and seasoning. Bring to a boil, reducing heat for 15-20 minutes, and simmer.

4. Add the boiling potatoes, then cook for another 15 minutes.

5. Cover it with bacon bits and chives.

6. Let it cool for the best flavor and reheat.

9. Gallagher's Cheddar Cheese Soup

Preparation time: In about 40 minutes

Servings: 8

Difficulty: Moderate

Ingredients:

- Two cups of water

- 1/3 cup finely chopped carrots

- 1/3 cup finely chopped celery

- One cup of finely chopped green onions

- Half cup butter

- A quarter cup all-purpose flour

- One cup of chopped white onion

- Four cups of milk

- Four cups of chicken broth

- 15 ounces pasteurized process cheese spread

- salt and pepper to taste

- A quarter teaspoon of Cayenne

- One tablespoon of Prepared mustard

Instructions:

1. Put water over high heat in a soup pot. Bring to a boil for 5 minutes; set aside, but do not drain. Add the carrots, celery and green onions.

2. Melt butter over medium heat in a broad stockpot and add onion; sauté for 1 minute, then add flour, mixing well.

3. Boil the milk and broth in a large saucepan. Whisk a paste of broth into a flour mixture with a wire whisk.

4. Stir in the cheese, salt, cayenne and pepper. Stir in the mustard and vegetables that have been cooked, plus the water in which they have been cooked. Bring it to a boil and immediately serve.

10. Huston's Canadian Cheese Soup

Preparation time: In about 55 minutes

Servings: 4 to 6

Difficulty: Moderate

Ingredients:

- Eight tablespoons of (one stick) butter or margarine

- One cup of finely diced carrots

- Half cup finely diced onion

- Half cup finely diced celery

- Two to Three tablespoons of all-purpose flour

- Three cups of half-and-half

- Three cups of chicken broth

- Two pounds Velveeta cheese, cut into cubes

Garnish

- One tablespoon of minced fresh parsley

- Diced tomatoes

- Diced jalapeño pepper

Instructions:

1. Heat the butter in a large saucepan and sauté the carrots, onion, and celery. Do not brown the vegetables; they are only meant to be fluffy. Whisk and mix in the flour for a minute or two, then add the half-and-a-half and boil over low heat. Don't let the mixture boil; once it is thickened, just let it simmer.

2. Add the chicken broth steadily, whisking up the mix to combine all the ingredients. Like a cream sauce, the broth can be slightly thickened. For around 10 minutes, let it boil, so the flour has a chance to cook.

3. Stir in the cheese until it is fully molten, continuously whisking. Garnish with the parsley and, if you prefer, the tomatoes and jalapeños with the soup in warmed cups.

11. MGM Grand Spicy Jambalaya

Preparation time: In about 56 minutes

Servings: 6

Difficulty: Moderate

Ingredients:

- Six bay leaves

- pounds diced ham

- Two gallons of water

- vegetable oil for sauteing

- Five pounds diced chicken breast

- Two pounds chopped onions

- Two pounds chopped onions

- One and a half pounds chopped green pepper

- One cup of chopped green onions

- Two pounds diced tomatoes

- Two cups of tomato paste

- Three tablespoons of chopped parsley

- Four ounces chopped garlic

- Two teaspoons of dried thyme

- Two teaspoons of cayenne pepper

- A quarter cup Worcestershire sauce

- Three pounds smoked sausage

- Three pounds of rice

- One tablespoon of salt

Instructions:

1. Add the bay leaves, chopped ham, and water to the boiler. Let boil for 1 hour. Heat the oil in another pan. Add the diced chicken, celery and onions. Sauté and add the peppers, onions and diced tomatoes until tender. Put in the tomato paste, chopped parsley, crushed garlic, dried thyme, Worcestershire sauce, cayenne pepper, and smoked sausage.

2. Fill the jambalaya with fried rice and add salt to taste.

12. Olive Garden's Italian Sausage Soup

Preparation time: In about 40 minutes

Servings: 4

Difficulty: Moderate

Ingredients:

- One pound of bulk sweet Italian sausage

- One cup of converted white rice

- Six cups of beef broth

- One cup of chopped tomatoes

- Two tablespoons of tomato paste

- Salt and pepper

- One 10-ounce box of frozen spinach, thawed, drained, and chopped

- Grated Pecorino Romano cheese for garnish

Instructions:

1. In a stockpot, sauté the sausage, breaking it up as it cooks. Add the rice until deeply browned and stir until it is completely covered in the sausage's fat. Bring to a boil, add beef broth, tomatoes, tomato paste, salt and 1/4 teaspoon of pepper.

2. Reduce the heat and simmer until the rice is tender, for 12 to 15 minutes. However, add the diced spinach to ensure that it is well-drained; if possible, squeeze it into a dish towel to keep the moisture out. For a few minutes, let the soup boil, then season with salt and pepper.

3. Add the soup too hot bowls and garnish with the brushed cheese.

13. Outback Steakhouse Walkabout Soup

Preparation time: In about 40 minutes

Servings: 4

Difficulty: Moderate

Ingredients:

- Two cups of thinly sliced yellow sweet onions

- Two tablespoons of butter

- 14– to 15–ounce can chicken broth

- A quarter teaspoon of salt

- A quarter teaspoon fresh ground pepper

- Two chicken bouillon cubes

- A quarter cup diced Velveeta cubes

- One and a half cups white sauce

- Shredded Cheddar cheese for garnish

Thick white sauce

- Three tablespoons of butter

- Three tablespoons of flour

- A quarter teaspoon of salt

- One and a half cups of whole milk

Instructions:

1. Make the white sauce first. For that, melt butter and add flour in a 1-quart saucepan; cook on medium heat until the flour becomes dense and comes from the side of the saucepan.

2. Pour a little milk into the flour mixture and constantly stir, taking care not to cause it to lump. Set aside (off the heat) in the broth until ready to use.

3. Add two tablespoons of butter and sliced onions in a 2-quart saucepan. Cook at low to medium heat, stirring regularly, but not brown, until smooth and clear.

4. Add a can of chicken broth, chicken bouillon cubes, salt, pepper, and mix until fully cooked.

5. Add the Velveeta cheese and white sauce. It would be dense with the white sauce since it has been separated from the sun. Simmer until the cheese is melted and all the ingredients are combined, stirring continuously, over medium-low heat.

6. Turn the heat to warm and let it cook for an extra 30 minutes. Serve with a garnish of sliced Cheddar cheese and a few hot dark Russian bread slices.

14. Panera Bread Broccoli Cheese Soup

Preparation time: In about 45 minutes

Servings: 4

Difficulty: Moderate

Ingredients:

- One tablespoon of butter, melted

- Half medium onion, chopped

- A quarter C. flour

- A quarter C. melted butter

- Two C. Half & Half

- Two C. chicken stock

- Half lb. fresh broccoli

- One C. carrots, julienned

- ¼ teaspoons of nutmeg

- salt and pepper, to taste

- Eight oz. grated sharp cheddar

Instructions:

1. In butter, sauté the onion. And put aside. Cook the melted butter and flour for around 4 minutes over medium heat using a whisk. Make sure to stir regularly. Add the half & half gently, stirring more.

2. Whisking all the time, add the chicken stock. For 20 minutes, boil it.

3. Add the broccoli, onions and carrots. Cook for about 20 minutes, over low heat, until the vegetables are soft. Incorporate salt and pepper. The broth should have thickened by now. Pour in the blender and puree into batches.

4. Place the puree back in the pot over low heat; add the grated cheese; whisk until well mixed. Stir the nutmeg in. Just serve.

15. Huston's Tortilla Soup

Preparation time: In about 1 hour 35 minutes
Servings: 4 to 6
Difficulty: Hard

Ingredients:

- One two and a half to three pounds of chicken, cut up, skin removed

- Two ribs celery, cut into chunks

- One medium onion, quartered

- One large carrot, quartered

- Two sprigs of fresh parsley

- Two tablespoons of chicken bouillon powder

- One teaspoon of lemon pepper

- One large clove of garlic, minced

- One and a half pounds potatoes, peeled

- One 14.75-ounce can cream-style corn

- One 10-ounce can Ro Tel tomatoes, crushed, with juice

- One and a half cups of half-and-half two to Four tablespoons of minced fresh cilantro

- Salt and black pepper

- One cup of shredded Cheddar cheese

- One cup of shredded Monterey Jack cheese

Garnish

- Sour cream

- Avocado, cut into chunks

- Black olives, pitted and sliced

- Four to Six corn tortillas, cut into ¼-inch strips and fried

Instructions:

1. In a big stockpot, put your chicken, celery, onion, carrot, and parsley. Then add the chicken bouillon powder, lemon pepper, and garlic and add enough water to cover 2 to 3 inches. Make sure it is well dissolved in the bouillon powder. On high heat, bring the pot to a boil, the heat and simmer for around 1 hour, or until the chicken is tender and the bones fall off. Strain the pot's contents and reserve the broth. Cut the meat and discard the bones and vegetables into bite-size pieces.

2. Boil four cups of the reserved chicken broth with the potatoes until they are tender. Using a potato masher, remove the pan from the heat and mash it together with their broth. Creamed corn, onions, half-and-a-half, and cilantro are added, blended and mixed well.

3. Heat the mixture of potatoes over low heat and boil, adding enough reserved broth for about 15 minutes to make a thick and fluffy soup. Add the salt and black pepper to taste, then stir in the diced chicken and the shredded cheese.

4. Ladle the soup with a dollop of sour cream, pieces of avocado, black olive slices, and tortilla strips into warmed bowls and garnish each serving.

Chapter 9: Salad Recipes

1. Applebee's Low-Fat Blackened Chicken Salad

Preparation time: In about 30 minutes
Servings: 2
Difficulty: Moderate

Ingredients:

Dressing

- A quarter C. fat-free mayonnaise
- A quarter C. Grey Poupon Dijon mustard
- A quarter C. honey
- One tablespoon of prepared mustard
- One tablespoon of white vinegar
- 1/8 teaspoon paprika
- Chicken Marinade:
- 1 C. water
- Three tablespoons of lime juice
- Two tablespoons of soy sauce
- Half tablespoon of Worcestershire

Cajun Spice Blend

- Half tablespoon of salt
- One teaspoon of sugar

- One teaspoon of paprika

- One teaspoon of onion powder

- One teaspoon of black pepper

- Half teaspoons of garlic powder

- Half teaspoons of cayenne pepper

- Half teaspoons of white pepper

- Two boneless, skinless chicken breast halves

- Two tablespoons of light butter

Salad

- Eight C. chopped iceberg lettuce

- Half C. shredded red cabbage

- Half C. shredded carrot

- Half C. fat-free shredded mozzarella cheese

- Half C. fat-free shredded cheddar cheese

- One large tomato, diced

- One hard-boiled egg white, diced

Instructions:

1. Make the dressing in a small bowl by mixing ingredients. Mix by hand well. Store in the refrigerator in a sealed container until the salad is ready.

2. In a medium bowl, mix the water, lime juice, soya sauce, Worcestershire, and whisk.

3. Apply the chicken breasts to the marinade, cover the bowl and leave for several hours in the refrigerator. It's much better overnight.

4. When the chicken is marinated, over medium/high heat, preheat a frying pan or skillet.

5. Preheat the barbecue grill to medium/high heat, as well.

6. Combine the ingredients in a small bowl with the Cajun spice blend. Sprinkle the spice blend with a teaspoon on one side of each of the chicken breasts.

7. Coat the chicken's whole surface with seasoning. In the hot pan, melt the butter and cook the chicken breasts with the spices on the side for 2-3 minutes.

8. Sprinkle another teaspoon of spice over the top of each chicken breast as the first side heats, covering the side as the first one did.

9. Flip over the chicken and sear for 2-3 more minutes. A charred, black coating of seasoning will cover the surface of the chicken.

10. For 2-3 minutes or until they are finished, grill each breast on both sides.

11. By separating the lettuce into two large bowls, prepare the salads while the chicken is frying. Toss in the carrots and red cabbage.

12. Mix the cheeses and add the cheeses and the hardboiled egg to the salad. Sprinkle each salad with a diced tomato.

13. In half-inch-thick parts, slice the chicken breast around each breast. Spread the chicken over the top of the salad and serve with dressing on the side immediately.

2. Famous Dave's Shakin' the Shack Potato Salad

Preparation time: In about 45 minutes

Servings: 6 to 8

Difficulty: Moderate

Ingredients:

- Three pounds russet potatoes, scrubbed

- One and a quarter cups of mayonnaise

- Half cup sour cream

- One tablespoon of yellow mustard

- One tablespoon of white vinegar

- One teaspoon of salt

- One teaspoon of sugar

- Half teaspoon pepper

- Half cup minced celery

- Half cup minced red onion

- Half cup minced green bell pepper

- Two tablespoons of minced pimiento

- One tablespoon of minced jalapeño pepper

- Five hard-cooked eggs, minced

- 1/4 cup pickle relish

- Paprika, for garnish

Instructions:

1. In the cookpot, add the potatoes and cover them with water. Boil it until it becomes tender and cooked but not mushy. Drain until cool, then refrigerate.

2. Add the mayonnaise, sour cream, mustard, vinegar, salt, sugar, and peppers in a large bowl and refrigerate until ready for use.

3. Peel the cold potato skins and chop them coarsely.

4. Put the celery, red onion, bell pepper, pimiento and jalapeño together. Add to the mixture of mayonnaise and fold in the potatoes, eggs and relish. Use paprika for garnish.

3. Chi-Chi's Mexican Chicken Salad

Preparation time: In about 20 minutes

Servings: 4

Difficulty: Easy

Ingredients:

- One cup of Chi-Chi's Salsa or store-bought salsa

- One pound of boneless, skinless chicken breasts, cooked and shredded

- Two hard-cooked eggs, finely chopped

- Half cup sour cream

- A quarter cup of mayonnaise

- Two tablespoons of minced onion

- One teaspoon of grated lime zest

- Half teaspoon chili powder

- 1/4 teaspoon ground cumin

- Lettuce leaves, for plate liners

Instructions:

1. Drain the salsa well—whether it's Chi-Chi's or some other, too much liquid will make the salad watery.

2. Put the salsa and all the remaining ingredients except the lettuce leaves and stir well to blend in a big bowl. Line 4 serving plates with lettuce leaves and mound the chicken salad on top of each.

4. Dave and Buster's Steak Fajita Salad

Preparation time: In about 45 minutes

Servings: 2

Difficulty: Moderate

Ingredients:

Buttermilk-Cilantro Dressing

- One 1-ounce package of buttermilk
- Ranch salad dressing mix
- Half cup mayonnaise
- Half cup sour cream
- ¼ cup buttermilk

- One cup of chopped fresh cilantro
- Two cloves garlic, minced
- ¼ teaspoon cayenne pepper, or to taste

Salad

- Eight ounces steak
- One 1.12-ounce package fajita seasoning mix
- Six ounces romaine hearts, chopped
- Half cup grated Cheddar cheese
- ¼ cup diced onion
- One cup of plain tortilla strips
- One large flour tortilla bowl

Garnish

- Sour cream
- Multicolored tortilla strips
- Two tablespoons of chopped fresh cilantro

Instructions:

1. Combine all the buttermilk-cilantro dressing ingredients in a blender and blend until smooth. Refrigerate until ready-to-use in a covered container.

2. Follow the guidelines for marinating the steak in the seasoning blend of the fajita.

3. Light up the barbecue with charcoal or preheat the broiler.

4. Drain the steak from the marinade to the perfect doneness, and grill or broil. Slice it up into even slices against the grain. Shift the marinade away.

5. Toss the cheese, onion, and plain tortilla strips with the romaine. Combine it with six tablespoons of salad dressing and cover the tortilla bowl. Top it with steak strips.

6. Top it with steak strips and garnish with sour cream, multicolored strips of tortilla, and cilantro.

5. Golden Corral's Seafood Salad

Preparation time: In about 1 hour 10 minutes
Servings: 4 to 8
Difficulty: Moderate

Ingredients:

- Eight ounces imitation crab meat, shredded

- One cup of small shrimp, peeled, deveined, and cooked

- One large green bell pepper, minced

- One medium onion, minced

- Half cup of ranch salad dressing

- 1⁄4 cup mayonnaise

- Lettuce leaves, for plate liners

Instructions:

1. Combine all the salad ingredients gently and refrigerate for 1 hour or so.

2. Mound it on lettuce-lined dressing salad plates.

6. Huston's Grilled Chicken Salad

Preparation time: In about 40 minutes

Servings: 4

Difficulty: Moderate

Ingredients:

Honey-Lime Dressing

- Half cup lime juice

- Four teaspoons of honey mustard

- Two cloves garlic, minced

- One teaspoon of pepper

- Half teaspoon salt

- ¼ cup plus Three tablespoons of honey

- Peanut Sauce

- ¼ cup soy sauce

- ¼ cup hot water

- ¼ cup creamy peanut butter

- Two teaspoons of Asian sesame oil

- One teaspoon of ground ginger

Salad

- One bag of mixed salad greens, chilled

- One large carrot, julienned and chilled

- Two grilled chicken breasts, cut into bite-size pieces and chilled

- Thin tortilla strips

Instructions:

1. Make the honey-lime dressing by mixing all the dressing ingredients thoroughly. Set aside or refrigerate in a closed container until ready to go.

2. Make the peanut sauce by whisking together all the ingredients thoroughly. Set aside or refrigerate in a closed container until ready to use, but take it to room temperature before use.

3. Toss the honey-lime dressing with all the salad ingredients and divide them into four salad plates. Drizzle the peanut sauce with it.

7. Chili's Grilled Caribbean Chicken Salad

Preparation time: In about 25 minutes

Servings: 4

Difficulty: Easy

Ingredients:

- Four boneless, skinless chicken breast halves

- Half cup of teriyaki marinade

- Four cups of chopped iceberg lettuce

- Four cups of chopped green leaf lettuce

- One cup of chopped red cabbage

- One oz. can pineapple chunks in juice, drained

- tortilla chips

Pico De Gallo

- Two medium tomatoes, diced

- Half cup of diced Spanish onion

- Two teaspoons of chopped fresh jalapeno pepper, seeded and de–ribbed

- Two teaspoons of finely minced fresh cilantro

- pinch of salt

Honey Lime Dressing

- A quarter cup Grey Poupon Dijon mustard

- A quarter cup of honey

- One and a half tablespoon of apple cider vinegar

- One and a half tablespoon of lime juice

- One and a half tablespoon of sugar

- One tablespoon of sesame oil

Instructions:

1. Combine all the ingredients in a small bowl to make Pico De Gallo. Chill and cover.

2. Blend all the ingredients in a small bowl with an electric blender for the Honey Lime Dressing. Chill and cover.

3. For at least two hours, marinate the chicken in the teriyaki. And use a resealable plastic bag. Place it in the fridge.

4. Preheat the grill and grill the chicken on either side or until cooked, for 4-5 minutes.

5. Toss together the lettuces and cabbage and split into two salad bowls of great serving size.

6. Divide the Pico de Gallo and dump over the two bowls of greens in equal parts. Divide the salads and sprinkle them with pineapple.

7. Break-in big pieces of tortilla chips and sprinkle them on a salad. The grilled chicken is cut into thin strips and separated into bowls.

8. Place the dressing in two small bowls and serve with the salad.

8. Applebee's Santa Fe Chicken Salad

Preparation time: In about 1 day and 35 minutes

Servings: 1

Difficulty: Hard

Ingredients:

Pico de Gallo

- Three large tomatoes, diced

- One large onion, diced

- Two tablespoons of diced jalapeño pepper

- Two teaspoons of salt

- Half teaspoon black pepper

- Half teaspoon garlic powder

- Half cup chopped fresh cilantro

- One tablespoon of olive oil

- One tablespoon of white vinegar

- One boneless chicken, skinless chicken breast

Chicken Marinade

- Two tablespoons of gold tequila

- 1/4 cup lime juice

- Two tablespoons of orange juice

- 3/4 teaspoon minced jalapeño pepper

- 3/4 teaspoon minced garlic

- ¼ teaspoon salt

- ¼ teaspoon black pepper

- One teaspoon of fajita seasoning mix

Mexican-Ranch Dressing

- ¼ cup mayonnaise

- ¼ cup sour cream

- One tablespoon of milk

- Two teaspoons of minced tomato

- Half teaspoon white vinegar

- One teaspoon of minced jalapeño pepper

- One teaspoon of minced onion

- ¼ teaspoon dried parsley

- ¼ teaspoon Tabasco sauce

- Pinch of salt

- Pinch of dried dill

- Pinch of paprika

- Pinch of cayenne pepper

- Pinch of ground cumin

- Pinch of chili powder

- Pinch of garlic powder

- Pinch of black pepper

- Mixed salad greens

Garnish

- Shredded Cheddar cheese

- Chopped green onions

- Crushed tortilla chips

- Sour cream, for serving

- Guacamole, for serving

Instructions:

1. Make the Pico de Gallo in a tightly closed container by mixing all the ingredients and refrigerating them overnight.

2. Marinate the chicken in a tightly covered container overnight by mixing all the marinade ingredients (except the fajita seasoning mix) and refrigerating, flipping the chicken regularly.

3. Make the dressing in a tightly covered container by carefully mixing all the ingredients and refrigerating.

4. Light up a charcoal grill or preheat the broiler when it's time to cook the salad.

5. Remove the chicken from the marinade, and the excess is to be shaken out. Use the reserved fajita seasoning mix, season both sides of the chicken and grill the chicken until cooked.

6. Get a bowl of your favorite mixed greens packed. Slice the chicken breast into small strips and put it on top of the greens. Garnish with melted cheddar, green onions and crushed tortilla chips over the top of the salad. Serve with Pico de Gallo ramekins, sour cream, then guacamole, and on the side with lots of Mexican-ranch dressing.

9. California Pizza Kitchen Waldorf Chicken Salad

Preparation time: In about 55 minutes

Servings: 2

Difficulty: Moderate

Ingredients:

Salad Dressing

- One cup of olive oil

- Half cup balsamic vinegar

- Two tablespoons of Dijon mustard

- One tablespoon of minced garlic

- Half teaspoon fresh ground black pepper

- 1/4 teaspoon salt

Salad

- Six cups of mixed baby greens

- Half cup diced celery

- One granny smith apple, chopped into bite-sized pieces

- Half cup halved red seedless grapes2 sliced grilled chicken breasts

- Half cup candied walnuts

- Crumbled gorgonzola cheese, to taste

Instructions:

1. In a bowl with a lid, whisk together all the dressing ingredients.

2. Before eating, cool the salad dressing and the plates in the refrigerator for 30 minutes.

3. Put together the greens, celery, and fruits and put them on the chilled plates.

4. Drizzle on the dressing for the salad.

5. Put chicken breast, candied walnuts, and gorgonzola on top of the salad.

10. Luby-Cafeteria's Green Pea Salad

Preparation time: In about 40 minutes

Servings: 8

Difficulty: Moderate

Ingredients:

- 32 ounces frozen green peas, thawed

- One cup of finely diced Cheddar cheese

- One cup of diced celery

- Half cup thinly sliced sweet pickle

- Half cup diced red bell pepper or pimiento

- Half cup mayonnaise

- Salt and pepper

- Lettuce leaves, for serving

Instructions:

1. Rinse the peas that are thawed and drain well. Put the remainder of the salad ingredients together and chill for 2 hours.

2. Line the lettuce leaf salad plates, top with the salad and serve.

11. Dave and Buster's Muffaletta Salad

Preparation time: In about 1 hour

Servings: 4

Difficulty: Moderate

Ingredients:

- 24 slices pepperoni

- Two ounces sliced salami

- Four ounces sliced ham

- Four ounces sliced turkey

- One cup of sliced celery

- Four tablespoons of chopped green onion

- One cup of roasted red peppers

- 1/4 cup sliced black olives

- Half cup chopped green salad olives

- One and 1/4 pounds spiral pasta

- Three tablespoons of Italian dressing

- One and a half cups of assorted lettuce

- 1/4 cup julienned spinach leaves

- One cup of diced Roma tomatoes

- One cup of Italian cheese blend

- 1/4 cup shredded Asiago cheese

Instructions:

1. Chop the pepperoni, salami, ham and turkey into thin strips. Put the meat in a large bowl with the salad.

2. To the dish, add the celery, green onions, and roasted peppers.

3. To the bowl, chop and add all types of olives.

4. Add the pasta that has been cooked.

5. On the pasta, pour the Italian dressing and gently toss everything together.

6. On a cold serving plate, place the assorted lettuce and spinach, leaving a space in the middle for the pasta salad.

7. Pile the mixture of the salad high in the middle of the plate.

8. Top the salad with tomatoes and cheese.

12. California Pizza Kitchen Wedge Salad

Preparation time: In about 30 minutes

Servings: 2

Difficulty: Moderate

Ingredients:

- One head iceberg lettuce Blue cheese dressing, to taste

- Two peeled and chopped hard-boiled eggs

- Six slices chopped cooked bacon

- Blue cheese crumbles to taste

- Half cup chopped tomatoes

Instructions:

1. On the lettuce head, cut off any brown or dark green leaves.

2. By tapping it on a countertop, extract the inside core.

3. Cut the lettuce head in two.

4. For the lettuce wedge to lay flat, trim the opposite ends.

5. Place the blue cheese sauce on top of the lettuce.

6. Add chopped bacon and eggs.

7. Use the blue cheese crumbles and tomatoes to conclude the salad.

13. KFC Bean Salad

Preparation time: In about 25 minutes

Servings: 6

Difficulty: Moderate

Ingredients:

- One (16-ounce) can of green beans
- One (16-ounce) can of wax beans
- One (16-ounce) can of kidney beans
- One medium small-diced green pepper
- One medium small-diced white onion
- Half cup vegetable oil
- Half cup cider vinegar
- 3⁄4 cup sugar
- One and a half teaspoons of salt
- Half teaspoon black pepper

Instructions:

1. Drain and rinse all the beans.
2. Combine all the ingredients in an airtight container
3. Marinate in the refrigerator, preferably 3–4 days.
4. After the refrigeration, savor whenever you like.

14. Applebee's Oriental Chicken Salad

Preparation time: In about 45 minutes

Servings: 1

Difficulty: Moderate

Ingredients:

Oriental Dressing

- Three tablespoons of honey

- One and a half tablespoon of rice wine vinegar

- A quarter C. mayonnaise

- One teaspoon of Grey Poupon Dijon mustard

- 1/8 teaspoon of sesame oil

Salad

- One egg

- Half C. milk

- Half C. flour

- Half C. corn flake crumbs

- One teaspoon of salt

- A quarter teaspoon of pepper

- One boneless, skinless chicken breast half

- 2-4 C. vegetable oil (for frying)

- Three C. chopped romaine lettuce

- One C. red cabbage

- One C. Napa cabbage

- Half carrot, julienne or shredded

- One green onion, chopped

- One tablespoon of sliced almonds

- 1/3 C. chow Mein noodles

Instructions:

1. Preheat the oil over medium heat in a deep-fryer or deep pan. You want the oil temperature to be about 350 degrees F.

2. Blend all the dressing ingredients with an electric mixer in a shallow bowl. While cooking the salad, place the dressing in the refrigerator to cool.

3. Beat the egg in a small, shallow bowl, add the milk, then mix well.

4. Combine the flour with the cornflake crumbs, salt and pepper in another bowl.

5. Slice the chicken breast into four to five long strips. Dip each chicken strip into the egg mixture first, then thoroughly cover each slice into the flour mixture.

6. Each chicken finger is to be fried for 5 minutes or until the coating has darkened to brown.

7. Toss the chopped romaine with the chopped red cabbage, Napa cabbage, and carrots and prepare the salad. Sprinkle on top of the lettuce with the cut green onion.

8. Sprinkle the almonds over the salad, then the noodles with chow Mein.

9. Slice the chicken into small chunks those of the size of a bite. Place the chicken in the middle of the salad, which forms a pile.

10. Serve on the side with salad dressing.

Chapter 10: Main Course Recipes

1. Applebee's Southwest Steak

Preparation time: In about 1 hour

Servings: 4

Difficulty: Moderate

Ingredients:

- Two (5.5 oz.) sirloin steaks, or your favorite cut

- Four shakes of blackened steak seasoning

- Half C. red peppers - julienne cut

- Half C. green peppers - julienne cut

- One C. yellow onion - julienne cut

- Butter, as per requirement

- salt, to taste

- pepper, to taste

- garlic, coarse, to taste

- One slice of cheddar cheese

- One slice Monterey jack cheese - sliced

Instructions:

1. To 550 degrees F, preheat the skillet or grill.

2. Shake blackened steak seasoning to optimum doneness on one side of meat and grill, turning halfway between "flips" on the grill to achieve "diamond" grill traces.

3. Slice the onions and peppers as the steak is cooking. Melt the butter with the onions and peppers and sauté.

4. Use salt, pepper, and garlic to season. Lower the heat and hold until the steak has cooked.

5. Top with cheese slices for the final minute of cooking the steak.

2. Boston Market Meat Loaf

Preparation time: In about 1 hour 15 minutes

Servings: 4

Difficulty: Moderate

Ingredients:

Meat Mixture

- One and a half lb. lean ground chuck

- Half C. minced onions

- Half teaspoons of garlic salt

- 3/4 C. drained diced tomatoes

- 3/4 C. Plain bread crumbs

- One Egg

Topping

- 3/4 C. tomato sauce

- Two tablespoons of sugar

Instructions:

1. Mix all of the first lists of ingredients once well mixed.

2. Put in a lightly oiled pan of bread and bake for 3/4 hour at 350 degrees F

3. Remove the extra oil from the oven and drain it from the pan.

4. Combine the tomato sauce and sugar and sprinkle over the meatloaf, and put it back in the oven to finish baking, depending on the oven, for about half an hour.

3. Claim Jumper's Roasted Pork Loin

Preparation time: In about 35 minutes

Servings: 2

Difficulty: Moderate

Ingredients:

- One cup of chopped mixed vegetables

- One tablespoon of olive oil

- ¼ cup salsa

- Two scoops of mashed potatoes

- ¼ cup chopped roasted red peppers, homemade or store-bought

- One teaspoon of chopped fresh cilantro

- Half cup mixed grated Cheddar and Monterey Jack cheese

- One 6- to 7-pound cooked pork loin

- Half cup barbecue sauce

- Half cup tortilla strips

- Two biscuits

Instructions:

1 Steam the vegetables until crisp-tender, for 2 to 3 minutes. And put aside.

2 In a pan, heat the oil and add the vegetables and sauté for a couple of seconds. Add and heat the salsa, then move it to a bowl.

3 Put the mashed potatoes, the roasted peppers, the coriander and the blended cheeses together. With a wooden spoon or rubber spatula, blend properly.

4 For the mashed potato mixture, top up the vegetable mixture. On each of the two warmed plates, placed a bowl of the veggie-potato mix. Put alongside the bowl a serving of pork loin, glaze with a little barbecue sauce, and top with the tortilla strips.

5 At the rim of the plate, place a warm biscuit and serve immediately.

4. Applebee's Santa Fe Stuffed Chicken

Preparation time: In about 1 hour 45 minutes

Servings: 4

Difficulty: Hard

Ingredients:

- Eight skinless, boneless chicken breasts
- One (8 oz. or larger) package Monterey Jack cheese,
- Half C. butter, melted
- One C. Italian seasoned bread crumbs
- One and a half tablespoon of grated Parmesan cheese
- Half teaspoons of salt
- Half teaspoons of ground cumin
- Half teaspoons of ground black pepper
- One small red bell pepper
- One small green bell pepper

Instructions:

1. Slice eight slices of each of the cheese and save part of it for the cheese sauce.

2. Place one breast of chicken between two sheets of paper with wax.

3. Working from the center to the edges of lb. With a meat mallet until it's shaped flat and rectangular. Repeat for the breasts that exist.

4. Wrap cheese around the flattened chicken breasts. Secure with uncooked spaghetti noodles or wooden picks.

5. Combine the parmesan cheese, bread crumbs, flour, cumin and pepper. In the melting butter and then in the bread crumb mixture, roll the secured chicken bits.

6. In a 13 x 9-inch baking dish, place the chicken breasts, but do not crowd them. Drizzle over all eight of the breasts with the remaining butter.

7. To bake later, refrigerate for 1 hour or freeze.

8. Bake for 25 to 30 minutes or until the chicken is cooked in a preheated 400-degree oven.

9. With butter and flour, make a roux. Add about one C. of milk and get it to a boil. Add the cheese and reduce the heat, stirring continuously so that the cheese doesn't melt. To thin out the cheese sauce, add more milk as needed.

10.   Bell peppers with dice. Pour a cheese sauce over the top when the chicken is cooked, and sprinkle it with diced peppers.

5. Bennigan's Smothered Chicken

Preparation time: In about 2 hours 30 minutes

Servings: 4

Difficulty: Hard

Ingredients:

- Chicken Marinade
- Boneless, Skinless Chicken Breasts
- One C. sliced onions
- One C. sliced mushrooms
- One teaspoon of hickory smoke flavor
- Three tablespoons of butter or margarine

- Four to eight slices of provolone cheese
- Four slices of cooked bacon

Chicken Marinade

- One teaspoon of basil leaves
- One tablespoon of garlic powder
- Three tablespoons of hickory smoke flavoring
- A quarter C. white cooking wine
- A quarter C. vegetable oil
- Half teaspoons of salt
- Half teaspoons of black pepper
- Two tablespoons of vinegar

Instructions:

1. Combine in a dish of all ingredients. Marinate the beef for 2 hours in a covered bowl or plastic bag.

2. Slice the onions and mushrooms while the chicken is marinating and fry the bacon.

3. In butter and hickory smoke, sauté the mushrooms and onions for 3 to 5 minutes, or until the onions are translucent but not brown and the mushrooms are tender.

4. Remove the chicken from the marinade and grill it for 10 minutes or so. Do not make the chicken overcooked. Preheat the oven to broil while grilling. Remove from the grill after the chicken is cooked and place in a shallow baking dish.

5. And use a strip of bacon to cover each breast, then Provolone cheese, then some sautéed onions and mushrooms. For 3 to 5 minutes or until the cheese is bubbly, broil.

6. Olive Garden Style Lasagna

Preparation time: In about 1 hour
Servings: 8
Difficulty: Moderate

Ingredients:

Alfredo Sauce

- Half lb. Sweet or salted butter

- oz. Heavy cream

- Fresh ground white pepper

- One and a half C. grated Fresh Parmesan

- Eighteen slices of Mozzarella cheese

Ricotta Mixture

- One pint of Ricotta cheese

- Two oz. of grated Romano

- Three oz. of shredded Mozzarella

- Two tablespoons of sliced Green onions

- Two teaspoons of chopped fresh parsley

- Half teaspoons of Salt

- 1/8 teaspoon of Black pepper

- A quarter teaspoon of Dried basil

- A quarter teaspoon of Dried oregano

- One and A quarter C. cooled Alfredo sauce

Vegetable Mixture

- Four C. Broccoli florets

- Two C. chopped Carrots

- Four C. of sliced Mushrooms

- Two C. of diced Red bell peppers

- One C. of diced Green bell pepper

- One C. of diced Yellow onion

- Two C. of sliced Zucchini

- Lasagna strips

Instructions:

1. In a 9x13 pan, set out ample dry lasagna strips to ensure you have enough to make three complete layers, with slight overlap on each layer. Remove the dry strips and cook until barely "al dente" and drain according to the box directions.

2. Heat the water in the bottom of a double boiler to a boil for the Alfredo Sauce. In the top pot, add butter, cream and pepper and heat until it is fully melted, then whisk in the Parmesan cheese until it is melted and combined. To cool, remove the top pot and set it aside.

3. Split the sauce into two separate servings. For use later, refrigerate one part.

4. Combine all the ingredients in a bowl and combine well with a rubber spatula for the Ricotta Cheese Mixture. Set aside at room temperature.

5. Combine all the veggies and mix well.

6. Brush the bottom and sides of a 9x13 baking dish with vegetable spray for assembling.

7. Spread out strips of cooked lasagna (about 4) to cover the whole rim. Spread one and a quarter C of the Ricotta mix over the strips.

8. Top with a veggie blend of eight C and spread out equally. Layout 9 of the slices of mozzarella for the veggie sheet to cover.

9. Repeat the layering here. Cover the second layer of lasagna strips with mozzarella slices and spread them evenly to end with one and a quarter C of ricotta cheese mix.

10.   Spray a sheet of foil with vegetable spray for cooking and firmly cover the baking dish with the foil, spraying the side down.

11. Bake for around an hour or until the internal temperature is 165 degrees F in a preheated oven at 375 degrees F.

12. Remove from the oven and allow to sit before cutting and serving for a few minutes, covered.

13. Heat the reserved amount of Alfredo Sauce just before serving, spoon the hot sauce over each lasagna slice as it is served.

7. Olive Garden Spaghetti Carbonara

Preparation time: In about 1 hour

Servings: 4

Difficulty: Moderate

Ingredients:

- A quarter C. flour

- A quarter C. butter

- One quart of milk

- 1/8 teaspoon pepper

- Half teaspoons of salt

- 24 slices bacon, extra thick

- A quarter C. olive oil

- Three C. mushrooms, sliced

- Six tablespoons of scallions, finely minced

- One lb. spaghetti, uncooked

- Two teaspoons of fresh parsley, finely chopped

- Half C. Parmesan cheese, freshly grated

Instructions:

1. Melt the butter over medium heat in a 4-quart big saucepan. Add the flour and cook for about 1 minute.

2. And use a wire whip to mix the milk, salt and pepper and stir vigorously until the mixture scarcely comes to a boil.

3. Reduce the flame and boil for 5 minutes, often whipping before thickening the sauce. Just keep it warm.

4. Cook the bacon until it's completely cooked. Drain on towels made of cloth. Break the pieces into a quarter of an inch and mix in the sauce.

5. Over medium heat, heat the olive oil in a large skillet. Add minced onions and sliced mushrooms and sauté until golden. Mix in the sauce.

6. Cook spaghetti according to directions from the box. Drain well and, along with the parsley, add to the sauce.

7. Blend well and move to a tray for serving. Serve directly with sprinkled parmesan cheese.

8. Olive Garden Pasta Con Zucchini

Preparation time: In about 40 minutes

Servings: 4

Difficulty: Moderate

Ingredients:

Sauce

- 1/3 C. olive oil
- One C. onion, chopped
- One lb. fresh mushrooms, divided
- One and a half teaspoon of garlic, minced
- Three C. tomatoes, crushed
- oz. canned tomatoes, diced and drained
- One and a half C. tomato puree
- One C. black olives, sliced, drained
- Two teaspoons of capers, drained
- Half teaspoons of dried oregano
- Half teaspoons of dried basil
- ¼ teaspoons of black pepper
- ¼ teaspoons of crushed red pepper
- Half teaspoons of fennel seeds
- Half teaspoons of salt

Zucchini

- Four large zucchinis, sliced lengthwise A quarter " thick
- Two tablespoons of olive oil
- Dried basil

- Dried oregano

- Salt and black pepper

- One lb. rigatoni, cooked

- Parmesan, grated

Instructions:

1. Cut half of the mushrooms into quarters to make the sauce and reserve.

2. Mince the remaining portion finely. Heat olive oil over medium heat in a heavy Dutch oven.

3. Add onion and minced mushrooms. Cook for 10 minutes or until the onions are very tender, stirring regularly. Add quarters of garlic and mushroom and simmer for 5 minutes, stirring continuously.

4. Add the remaining ingredients, stir and simmer. Reduce the heat and boil, stirring regularly, for 20 minutes.

5. Sprinkle the sliced zucchini with salt, pepper, basil and oregano to make zucchini. Heat one tablespoon olive oil over medium heat in a large skillet. Place the slices of zucchini in a thin layer in the pan.

6. Sauté on either side for about 3 minutes, just until tender. Remove to a hot dish and cover to stay warm while the remaining zucchini is sautéed. When required, add the remaining olive oil. Sauce with ladles over pasta.

7. Top with slices of zucchini and serve. Pass in the extra Parmesan cheese and sauce.

9. Olive Garden Toasted Ravioli

Preparation time: In about 40 minutes

Servings: 4 to 6

Difficulty: Moderate

Ingredients:

- One 16 oz. Package of meat-filled ravioli (fresh or frozen, unthaw if frozen)

- Two eggs, beaten

- A quarter C. water

- One teaspoon of garlic salt

- One C. flour

- One C. bread crumbs plain

- One teaspoon of Italian seasoning

Instructions:

1. Mix eggs with water and beat well; set aside. Mix the bread crumbs with Italian seasonings and garlic salt and set them aside. In a cup, measure the flour and set it aside.

2. For deep frying, heat the vegetable oil in a deep fryer or skillet to 350 degrees F.

3. Dip the ravioli in the flour, wash the eggs, put them in the bread crumbs, and place them carefully in the hot oil.

4. Remove from the oil and drain. Fry until golden.

5. Serve with marinara sauce of your preference.

10. Olive Garden Spaghetti Delle Rocca

Preparation time: In about 40 minutes

Servings: 2 to 4

Difficulty: Moderate

Ingredients:

- One oz. extra-virgin olive oil

- One tablespoon of minced fresh garlic

- Two oz. washed and dried quartered button mushrooms

- Two oz. diced yellow onions

- Two lb. cherry tomatoes cut in half

- Half C. pitted Kalamata black olives

- Half C. pitted green olives

- Two teaspoons of capers, rinsed

- A quarter C. chopped fresh basil

- One tablespoon of minced fresh parsley

- Half teaspoons of salt

- A quarter teaspoon of crushed red pepper flakes

- One lb. dry pasta, cooked according to package instructions

- Grated Parmesan cheese to taste

Instructions:

1. In a saucepan, heat the oil. Garlic, onions and mushrooms are then added. For one minute, cook; do not brown.

2. Add cherry tomatoes, olives, capers, basil, parsley, salt and pepper; sauté for 10 minutes, stirring constantly. Combine the sauce and the drained pasta in a large bowl when they are still hot.

3. Garnish with fresh basil leaves; finish with grated Parmesan cheese.

11. El Pollo Loco Chicken

Preparation time: In about 35 minutes

Servings: 2 to 4

Difficulty: Moderate

Ingredients:

- A quarter cup of corn oil
- A quarter cup melted butter
- A quarter cup onion, minced
- Two tablespoons of garlic, finely minced
- Two to three drops of yellow food coloring
- A quarter teaspoon of ground cumin
- One teaspoon of dried oregano
- Four tablespoons of fresh lemon juice
- Four tablespoons of fresh orange juice
- One halved chicken, Two and a half to three pounds

Instructions:

1. In a large shallow pan, mix the oil, butter, onion, garlic, food coloring, cumin, lemon and orange juice.

2. Add the chicken halves and transform well to coat. Cover and marinate overnight or for several hours.

3. Remove the chicken from the marinade, then cook on the barbecue grill over medium coals, or in a broiler 4 inches underneath the heat, until the meat is browned on both sides and cooked, turning and occasionally basting, around 25 minutes.

4. Split the chicken into pieces.

5. Serve with rice and beans, tortillas with corn or flour, and fresh salsa.

12. Chi–Chi's Baked Chicken Chimichangas

Preparation time: In about 1 hour

Servings: 2 to 4

Difficulty: Moderate

Ingredients:

- Two and a half cups chicken, cooked, shredded

- Two tablespoons of olive oil

- Half cup of onion, chopped

- Two garlic cloves, minced

- Half tablespoon chili powder

- 16 ounces salsa

- Half teaspoon cumin

- Half teaspoon cinnamon

- pinch of salt

- 6 to 10-inch flour tortillas, nice flexible ones; if stiff, warm before filling

- One cup of refried beans

- Olive oil (for basting)

- Sour Cream

- Guacamole

Instructions:

1. Sauté the onion and garlic in oil in a broad saucepan until tender.

2. Stir in the chili powder, cumin, cinnamon and salsa. Stir in the chicken that is shredded. Let it cool. Heat the oven to 450.

3. x 10 x 1 baking pan, rimmed with oil. Spoon a heaping tablespoon of beans down the middle of each tortilla by starting with one tortilla.

4. Top the chicken mixture with a scant half cup. Fold up the tortilla back, top and sides; secure if necessary, with wooden toothpicks.

5. Place the chimichangas, seam side down, in a greased baking tray. With the grease, brush both edges.

6. Bake for 20 to 25 minutes or until brown and crispy golden brown, rotating every 5 minutes.

7. Use sour cream and guacamole to serve.

13. Olive Garden's Scaloppini Romana

Preparation time: In about 25 minutes

Servings: 2 to 4

Difficulty: Easy

Ingredients:

- One lb. veal scaloppini

- Half C. flour

- A quarter C. butter

- Six tablespoons of white wine

- Half tablespoon of chopped fresh rosemary

- Two medium tomatoes, diced

- Eight oz. blanched green beans

- Two oz. shaved Parmesan cheese

- salt and pepper, to taste

Instructions:

1. In flour, dredge the veal. Heat the butter in the pan. Add the veal and cook for 2 minutes; turn and add the tomatoes and beans, salt, pepper, and rosemary.

2. Cook for 2 minutes, add the wine and cook for 1-2 minutes.

3. Move to a plate for serving and finish with cheese.

14. Olive Garden Style Shrimp Cristoforo

Preparation time: In about 40 minutes

Servings: 4

Difficulty: Moderate

Ingredients:

Basil Butter

- Two oz. Fresh basil leaves

- Ten oz. Butter softened

- One teaspoon of Garlic, minced

- A quarter teaspoon of Salt

- 1/8 teaspoon of Black pepper

- Three tablespoons of Grated Parmesan cheese plus

- One tablespoon of Grated Romano cheese

Pasta

- One lb. Fresh linguine or angel hair pasta

- One lb. Medium shrimp, shelled

Instructions:

1. Remove any large basil stems and wash the leaves. Shake out the remaining water with a paper towel and wipe. Place in a food processor and process until finely chopped using the blade attachment process.

2. To get a uniformly chopped basil, process in two batches if necessary. Delete and reserve from the processor.

3. In a shallow mixer bowl, add butter. Whip the butter until it is pliable, using an electronic blender.

4. Add the garlic, salt, pepper, Romano and Parmesan cheese, and basil; combine until well combined.

5. Basil butter can be used instantly or preserved for 3 to 4 days, wrapped in the refrigerator.

6. According to package directions, cook pasta, drain well and keep warm.

7. Melt some basil butter over medium heat in a large skillet.

8. Add the shrimp and sauté for about 2 to 3 minutes, until done. Serve over pasta cooked hot.

9. Serve with freshly grated Parmesan cheese.

15. CPK Broccoli and Sun–Dried Tomato Fusilli

Preparation time: In about 30 minutes

Servings: 2 to 4

Difficulty: Moderate

Ingredients:

- One pound of dry fusilli pasta

- Half cup of extra virgin olive oil

- One teaspoon of salt

- A quarter cup chopped fresh garlic

- Two tablespoons of chopped fresh thyme leaves

- About 12 oil–packed sun–dried tomatoes

- drained and thinly sliced

- One quart of blanched broccoli florets, drained

- One cups of grated parmesan cheese and ¼ cup for garnish

Instructions:

1. Bring a huge pot to a boil with salted water. Pasta is cooked until al dente, 8 to 10 minutes.

2. Heat olive oil over high heat in a large non-stick frying pan.

3. Add salt and garlic; add thyme and sun-dried tomatoes as the garlic starts to tan. Add broccoli and toss.

4. Add drained pasta as the broccoli is cooked through.

5. Add one cup of all of the parmesan cheese, sprinkle and stir to combine.

6. Serve with a fresh dusting of parmesan cheese in warm bowls.

16. Stouffer's Grandma's Chicken and Rice Bake

Preparation time: In about 1 hour 25 minutes

Servings: 2 to 4

Difficulty: Moderate

Ingredients:

- One and a half pounds boneless, skinless chicken breasts

- Three cups of instant whole grain brown rice

- Two and a half cups water or broth

- One tablespoon of olive oil, divided

- Half cup chopped onion

- Two carrots, finely diced

- One cup of frozen peas

- 18-ounce can cream of mushroom soup

- Ten and a half ounce can cream of chicken soup

- Ten and a half ounce can cheddar cheese soup

- Two cups of milk

- Eight ounces shredded cheddar or three-cheese blend

- salt and pepper

- One and a half cups Panko-style bread crumbs

- Two tablespoons of butter, melted

- Half tablespoon paprika

Instructions:

1. Preheat the oven to 350°F. Use cooking spray to spray baking dishes or disposable pans.

2. Place the chicken in a 3-quart saucepan and cover it with water. Season lightly with salt and bring to a boil, simmer over low heat and cook for 20 minutes or until the chicken is scarcely cooked (it will finish in the oven).

3. With two forks, remove chicken and dice or shred; you should have about four cups.

4. Strain and measure the liquid. To make two and a half cups, add additional water, if necessary. Place it in the same pot again and get it to a boil. Lower the heat, add the rice and cover. Cook for 5 minutes, then turn the heat off and steam for an additional 5 minutes in the covered pan until the remaining Ingredients: are assembled.

5. Place half the olive oil and the chicken parts in a large non-stick skillet over medium-high heat. Just stir and cook until the chicken on the edges starts to tan. Remove the chicken and set it aside. In the same skillet, put the remaining oil and the onion and carrots.

6. Cook and stir for about 4 minutes until the carrots are tender and the onion is translucent. Add the peas, then remove them from the heat.

7. Combine the three soups, the cream, and the cheese in a large bowl. Stir in the chicken, the rice, and the vegetables gently. To taste, add salt and pepper, and spoon into prepared casseroles.

8. Stir together the bread crumbs, melted butter, then paprika and sprinkle over the casseroles evenly.

9. Bake for 40-45 minutes.

10. In the pans, let the mixture cool down completely. Wrap the plastic wrap over the whole pan and then wrap it with foil. Label and freeze.

11. Thaw in the refrigerator overnight until preparing to bake, and then bring to room temperature before unwrapping and baking as above.

17. The Olive Garden's Capellini Primavera

Preparation time: In about 45 minutes

Servings: 4 to 6

Difficulty: Moderate

Ingredients:

- Half C. (1 stick) butter

- One and a half C. chopped onions

- 3/4 C. julienne-cut carrots (1/8x1/8x1 Half -inch)

- Five C. broccoli florets, cut into 1-inch pieces

- Three C. sliced mushrooms

- One and A quarter C. thinly sliced yellow squash

- One teaspoon of minced garlic

- One and a half C. water

- One tablespoon of beef bouillon granules (or vegetable broth)

- A quarter C. sun-dried tomatoes, oil-packed, minced

- One and A quarter C. crushed tomatoes in puree

- One tablespoon of finely chopped fresh parsley

- A quarter teaspoon of dried oregano

- A quarter teaspoon of dried rosemary

- 1/8 teaspoon crushed red pepper flakes

- One lb. fresh angel-hair pasta

- Half C. grated Parmesan cheese

Instructions:

1. Over medium heat, melt the butter in a Dutch oven. Sauté the onions, carrots and broccoli for 5 minutes in the butter. Add the onions, garlic and squash. Sauté for two minutes.

2. Excluding pasta and cheese, add all the remaining ingredients; mix well.

3. Bring to a boil, then cook for 8-10 minutes or until soft and well blended with vegetables and flavors. Serve over cooked pasta.

4. Top with Parmesan.

18. TGI Friday's Bruschetta Chicken Pasta

Preparation time: In about 1 hour 15 minutes

Servings: 2 to 4

Difficulty: Hard

Ingredients:

Pasta

- One lb. angel hair pasta
- Two tablespoons of salt

Balsamic Glaze

- One C. balsamic vinegar
- One tablespoon of sugar
- Fresh Tomato Sauce:
- Six to eight medium-size Roma tomatoes
- Two tablespoons of olive oil
- A quarter teaspoon of salt
- 1/8 teaspoon of black pepper
- Two cloves of minced garlic
- Ten fresh basil leaves
- Half C. plain tomato sauce

Garlic Bread

- One stick of butter (A quarter lb.)

- 1/8 teaspoon salt

- 1/8 teaspoon black pepper

- 1/8 teaspoon garlic powder

Chicken

- Four 4-oz. chicken breasts

- salt and black pepper

- Two tablespoons of olive oil

- Two cloves garlic, thinly sliced

Instructions:

1. Cook the pasta first. For that, cook the pasta in half a gallon of salted water until al dente. Drain and transfer to a bowl. Place in an ice bath to cool, extract from the water and toss with two teaspoons of salad oil if prepared ahead of time.

2. Put all the ingredients together for the balsamic glaze, bring them to a boil in a small saucepan and turn down the flame to a simmer. Reduce by 75 percent and keep at room temperature until the sauce develops to a thick syrup.

3. Wash, core and dice tomatoes to a quarter of pieces for the tomato sauce, save juices and put in a small bowl. Wash, dry and slice basil leaves into thin strips. Add salt and pepper to tomatoes and keep for 2 hours before using.

4. Melt butter in the microwave for Garlic Bread and stir to combine seasonings. Drizzle your favorite bread with garlic butter and bake until crispy and golden brown at 350 degrees F (approximately 4 minutes).

5. For chicken, just before serving, grill the chicken breasts. Season the chicken breasts with salt on both sides and black pepper. For grill marks, grill 3-4 minutes per side, or until the chicken breasts exceed 165 degrees F

6. When you're done with all the above, heat a big saucepan under a medium-low flame, add two teaspoons of olive oil, then add the milk and heat them for about 20 seconds on a medium-low flame. Add two tablespoons of olive oil and heat oil for 20 seconds.

7. To the saucepan, add some leftover garlic butter from the bread. Sauté the garlic on either side in oil for 45 seconds until tender and smooth - do not brown the garlic.

8. Add the tomato mixture, raise the heat, and stir.

9. Add Half C. of plain tomato sauce to the pan and bring to a light boil.

10. In a saucepan, add the pasta and toss it with the fresh sauce.

11. Pass to a serving platter or tray and garnish with balsamic glaze.

12. Slice the chicken breast into strips and put it on top of the pasta.

13. Garnish with sliced fresh parsley.

19. Olive Garden Pollo Limone

Preparation time: In about 55 minutes

Servings: 2 to 4

Difficulty: Moderate

Ingredients:

- Four boneless skinless chicken breasts

- Three tablespoons of flour

- One and a half tablespoons olive oil

- A quarter C. finely chopped green onions

- Two minced cloves of garlic

- Half C. chicken broth

- A quarter C. dry white wine

- Two tablespoons of fresh lemon juice

- Two tablespoons of chopped fresh parsley

- One tablespoon of grated lemon peel

- salt and pepper

- One lb. chicken to A quarter-inch thick and sprinkle with salt and pepper

Instructions:

1. Set the flour in a bowl. Heat one teaspoon of oil over high heat in a nonstick skillet.

2. Cover the chicken lightly with flour and transfer to the skillet and cook until brown, for about 2 minutes per side.

3. Place the chicken on a plate and keep it warm. Heat half a teaspoon of olive oil over low heat in the same skillet.

4. Add the garlic and green onions; sauté until tender. Stir in the broth and wine, and scrape the brown bits out of the pan. Add two teaspoons of chopped parsley and lemon juice.

5. Bring to a boil and heat up to high, simmering for about 3 minutes. Mix in the lemon peel and season with salt and pepper to taste.

6. Return the chicken to the skillet and boil in the sauce until heated.

7. Place the chicken on a pan, spoon the juices over the chicken and add the remaining parsley.

20. Maccaroni Grill's Scaloppine Di Pollo

Preparation time: In about 40 minutes

Servings: 2 to 4

Difficulty: Moderate

Ingredients:

Lemon Butter Sauce

- Four Ounces lemon juice
- Two Ounces white wine
- Four Ounces heavy cream
- One Pound butter (4 sticks)

Chicken

- Six to eight chicken breasts (3–ounces each) pounded thin
- Oil and butter for sauteing chicken
- Two and 3/4 cups of flour, seasoned with salt and pepper, for dredging
- Six Ounces pancetta, cooked
- Twelve Ounces mushrooms, sliced
- Twelve Ounces artichoke hearts, sliced
- One tablespoon of capers
- One Pound Capellini pasta, cooked
- chopped parsley for garnish

Instructions:

1. Heat the lemon juice and white wine in a saucepan over medium heat to make the sauce. Bring it to a simmer and reduce it by a third.

2. Mix in the milk and boil until the mixture thickens (3 to 4 minutes). Add butter slowly until it is fully immersed.

3. With salt and pepper, season. Remove from heat and keep warm.

4. Cook and rinse the pasta. In a large pan, melt a tiny amount of oil and two teaspoons of butter.

5. Dredge the chicken in the flour and sauté in the pan until brown and cooked through, turning once. Remove the chicken from the pan.

6. The remaining Ingredients: are to be added to the pan. Heat until the mushrooms are cooked and tender. Add the chicken to the pan again.

7. To serve, put on each plate, the cooked pasta. To the chicken mixture, add half of the butter sauce and toss. Taste and adjust. If needed, add more sauce.

8. Set the mixture of chicken over the pasta. To each one, add a little more sauce.

9. Use parsley to garnish.

21. Claim Jumper's Pot Roast and Vegetables

Preparation time: In about 40 minutes

Servings: 2

Difficulty: Moderate

Ingredients:

Vegetables

- Half cup chopped carrots

- Half cup chopped turnip

- Half cup chopped sweet potato

- One medium onion, chopped

- Assorted chopped fresh herbs (thyme, rosemary, oregano)

- Olive oil

- Salt and pepper

Herb Gravy

- One clove garlic, chopped

- 1/4 cup chopped shallots

- Half cup fresh herbs, chopped

- Two tablespoons of olive oil

- One cup of beef broth or store-bought au jus mix

Roast

- ounces fully cooked chuck roast, cut into 1-inch cubes

- Mashed potatoes, for serving

Instructions:

1. Preheat the oven to 375°F.

2. Roast the vegetables in a little olive oil with the fresh herbs until they are caramelized. Season with salt and pepper and leave to cool and refrigerate until ready for use in a sealed container.

3. Sauté the garlic, shallots, and fresh herbs in olive oil to make the herb gravy. Add the broth of beef and boil for 5 minutes or so; set aside.

4. Place the cubed meat with the roasted vegetables and herb gravy in a skillet and simmer just to heat it.

5. With mashed potatoes, serve.

22. Chili's Spicy Garlic-and-Lime Shrimp

Preparation time: In about 45 minutes

Servings: 4

Difficulty: Moderate

Ingredients:

Seasoning Mix

- One teaspoon of salt
- ¼ teaspoon black pepper
- ¼ teaspoon cayenne pepper
- ¼ teaspoon parsley flakes
- Pinch of garlic powder
- ¼ teaspoon paprika
- Pinch of dried thyme
- Pinch of onion powder

Shrimp

- Two tablespoons of butter
- One clove garlic, chopped
- 24 large shrimp, peeled and deveined
- One lime

Instructions:

1. Combine and set aside the ingredients for the seasoning mix.

2. In a skillet, melt the butter. Sauté 10 seconds of the garlic and add the shrimp. Over the shrimp, squeeze the lime juice and scatter with the seasoning mix.

3. Sauté for 5 to 8 minutes until the shrimp is pink and fried.

23. Olive Garden's Risotto Milanese

Preparation time: In about 45 minutes

Servings: 4

Difficulty: Moderate

Ingredients:

- ¼ cup olive oil

- Half cup finely chopped onion

- Half teaspoon ground turmeric

- Half cup sliced mushrooms

- Five cups of chicken or vegetable broth

- One and a half cups of Arborio rice

- Half cup white wine

- Half cup grated Parmesan cheese

- Two tablespoons of butter

- Salt and pepper

- Fresh parsley sprigs, for garnish

Instructions:

1. Heat the olive oil over medium heat in a stockpot and sauté the onion and turmeric until the onion is tender. Add the mushrooms and sauté until some of the moisture is consumed.

2. In a saucepan, heat the broth and keep it warm.

3. Add the rice to the sautéed vegetables and stir until the olive oil mixture coats all the grains. Add the white wine and allow it to evaporate, stirring often.

4. Add the warm broth, half a cup at a time, allowing it to be absorbed, continuously stirring after each addition. Repeat this process until the rice is al dente, and all the broth is drained.

5. Remove the pan from the heat and add the Parmesan cheese and the butter. With each addition, mix gently. With salt and pepper, season.

6. Transfer and garnish with parsley in a warmed serving bowl.

24. Dave and Buster's Blackened Chicken Pasta

Preparation time: In about 45 minutes

Servings: 2

Difficulty: Moderate

Ingredients:

Cajun Blackening Spice

- ¼ cup paprika

- Three tablespoons of garlic powder

- Two tablespoons of celery salt

- One tablespoon of onion powder

- One tablespoon of ground cumin

- One teaspoon of cayenne pepper

- One teaspoon of dried thyme

- One teaspoon of chili powder

- Chicken and Pasta Sauce

- One tablespoon of olive oil

- Six ounces boneless, skinless chicken breast, cut into bite-size pieces

- One cup of sliced mushrooms

- Two teaspoons of Paul Prudhomme's Poultry Magic

- One teaspoon of minced garlic

- 1/3 cup diced Roma tomatoes, plus extra for garnish

- ¼ cup Alfredo sauce, homemade or store-bought

- One and a half cups heavy cream

- One and a half tablespoons of grated Asiago cheese

For Serving

- Eight ounces linguine, cooked according to the package Instructions:

- One teaspoon of chopped fresh parsley

Instructions:

1. Combine all the ingredients to make the Cajun blackening spice; store until ready to use in a tightly covered container.

2. In a pan, heat the oil and sauté the chicken and mushrooms. Sprinkle and cook the chicken all the way through with the Poultry Magic. Garlic and diced tomatoes are then to be added and sautéed for another minute.

3. Lower the heat and add two teaspoons of the Alfredo sauce, the Cajun blackening spice and the heavy cream.

4. To combine the ingredients, stir well and then take the pan off the heat and add the Asiago cheese.

5. Using tongs, serve the cooked linguine on two warmed serving plates and swirl and mound the pasta on each plate. Top with the chicken and sauce.

6. Garnish with diced tomato and sprinkle with the chopped parsley.

Chapter 11: Other Sides and Sauces Recipes

1. Boston Market Cornbread

Preparation time: 4 In about 5 minutes

Servings: 1

Difficulty: Moderate

Ingredients:

- One box Jiffy Mix Cornbread Mix

- One box Jiffy Mix Yellow Cake Mix

Instructions:

1. Mix both boxes according to instructions and combine the batter. Pour batter into an 8-inch square baking pan.

2. Bake at 350 degrees F until done. It takes about 30 minutes.

2. Houston's Spinach and Artichoke Dip

Preparation time: In about 45 minutes

Servings: 1

Difficulty: Moderate

Ingredients:

- Two bags (1 lb. each) of fresh spinach

- 1/8 lb. butter – not margarine

- One teaspoon of minced fresh garlic

- Two tablespoons of minced onions

- A quarter cup flour

- One pint of heavy cream (whipping cream)

- Two teaspoons of freshly-squeezed lemon juice

- Half teaspoon of Tabasco sauce (to taste)

- Half teaspoon of salt

- 2/3 cup fresh grated Parmesan cheese

- 1/3 cup sour cream

- Half cup of grated Monterey Jack cheese

- artichoke hearts, coarsely diced

Instructions:

1. Steam spinach through a cheesecloth, strain and pinch. It's got to be dry. Finely chop and set aside.

2. Melt the butter in a large saucepan.

3. Add onions and garlic and sauté for around 3-5 minutes.

4. To make a roux, add flour. For around 1 minute, stir and cook. Heavy cream is applied gently, swirling with a whisk to avoid lumping. At the boiling point, the liquid will thicken.

5. Add lemon juice, Tabasco, salt and Parmesan cheese when it thickens.

6. Remove from the heat and leave it to stand for five minutes. Stir together the sour cream.

7. Fold in dry, minced spinach, Jack's cheese and coarsely sliced artichoke hearts. Stir until you've melted the cheese.

8. Serve promptly, or microwave before serving. For dipping, serve with mustard, sour cream and tortilla chips.

3. Famous Dave's Barbecue Sauce

Preparation time: In about 45 minutes

Servings: 10 cups

Difficulty: Moderate

Ingredients:

- Two slices thick-cut hickory-smoked bacon, chopped
- ¼ cup chopped onion
- ¾ cup peach schnapps
- Half cup raisins
- One large jalapeño pepper, finely diced
- Two cloves garlic, minced
- 1/3 cup Alessi balsamic vinegar
- ¼ cup chopped apple
- ¼ cup frozen tangerine juice concentrate or orange juice concentrate
- ¼ cup frozen pineapple juice concentrate
- Three tablespoons of dark molasses
- Two tablespoons of apple cider vinegar
- Two tablespoons of lemon juice
- Two tablespoons of lime juice
- Two and ¼ cups of dark corn syrup
- One 12-ounce can of tomato paste
- Half cup packed light brown sugar
- Half cup Worcestershire sauce
- Two tablespoons of yellow mustard
- Two teaspoons of chili powder
- One teaspoon of Maggi seasoning

- One teaspoon of salt
- Half teaspoon red pepper flakes
- 1/4 teaspoon coarsely ground black pepper
- One teaspoon of cayenne pepper
- 1/4 cup Kahlua
- One teaspoon of liquid smoke

Instructions:

1. Over medium heat, sauté the bacon in a large saucepan to make the fat (save the bacon bits for another use). You should have one tablespoon of bacon drippings.

2. Sauté the onion until it is caramelized to rich golden color in the bacon fat. Reduce the heat to low, and 1/4 cup of water will deglaze the saucepan.

3. Then add the raisins, jalapeño, and garlic and whisk in the peach schnapps. Simmer, stirring regularly, for about 20 minutes, or until the syrup has the mixture's consistency.

4. Remove from the heat and set aside, or cool and refrigerate until ready for use in a covered container.

5. In a mixer, transfer the onion mixture and add the balsamic vinegar, diced apple, tangerine, concentrated pineapple juice, molasses, apple cider vinegar, lemon, lime juice, etc.

6. Process and return to the saucepan until pureed. Add the corn syrup, tomato paste, light brown sugar, Worcestershire sauce, mustard, chili powder, Maggi salt, black pepper, red pepper flakes, and cayenne pepper. Simmer for about 20 minutes on a low flame, stirring periodically.

7. Remove from the heat and stir in the Kahlua and liquid smoke.

8. Let it cool, then refrigerate until ready for use in a covered container.

4. Steak & Ale's Burgundy Mushrooms

Preparation time: In about 30 minutes

Servings: 1

Difficulty: Easy

Ingredients:

- One and A quarter pounds of mushrooms
- Two quarts water
- A quarter cup lemon juice
- Four tablespoons of margarine
- 3/4 cup yellow onions, diced
- Half cup of Burgundy
- One tablespoon of beef bouillon granules
- A quarter teaspoon garlic powder
- 1/3 teaspoon ground white pepper

Instructions:

1. Clean and dry the mushrooms. Combine in a closed saucepan, water and lemon juice. Just bring it to a boil.

2. Melt the margarine in another saucepan and sauté the onions until they are glassy (about 5 minutes).

3. Add the spices and bouillon to the Burgundy in a bowl. Whisk until there is a dissolved bouillon.

4. Add a mixture of wine to the onions. Simmer for approximately 10 minutes over the medium sun (until the alcohol has evaporated). Suspend from the heat.

5. Add the boiling lemon water to the mushrooms. Return to the boil. Remove the whitened mushrooms from the heat and rinse thoroughly.

6. Add the wine sauce to the mushrooms and stir until combined.

5. Golden Corral's Rolls

Preparation time: In about 50 minutes

Servings: 24 rolls

Difficulty: Moderate

Ingredients:

- On envelope (2¼Four teaspoons of) active dry yeast
- ¼ cup warm water (105° to 115°F)
- 1/3 cup sugar Six tablespoons of (¾ stick) unsalted butter, plus extra for the pan
- One teaspoon of salt
- One cup of hot milk
- One egg, beaten

- Four and a half cups of all-purpose flour sifted

Instructions:

1. Sprinkle the yeast over the warm water in a wide bowl and leave to proof for around 5 minutes.

2. Combine the sugar, Four tablespoons of butter, salt, and hot milk in another bowl. Until the butter is molten and the sugar is dissolved, whisk with a wooden spoon. Let the mixture cool to 105 ° to 115 ° F, then apply it along with the beaten egg to the proofed yeast mixture.

3. One cup at a time, add the flour, combining well after each addition. Shape the dough into a softball after the fourth cup. Sprinkle on a work surface with some of the remaining half cup flour and knead the dough for around 5 minutes, steadily focusing on all the remaining flour.

4. Oil the inside of a bowl, gently and place the dough in it, flipping it over once so that both sides are oiled. Cover it with a damp towel and set the bowl free from drafts in a warm area.

5. Punch it flat, roll it out onto a lightly floured work surface and knead for 4 to 5 minutes until the dough has doubled in size, 1 to 1 half hours. Set aside and butter an 18 by a 13-inch baking pan.

6. Tiny amounts of dough are pinched off and molded into balls. One and a half to one and 3/4 inches wide until you have 24 rolls.

7. In the prepared baking pan, position the rolls so that they do not hit one another. Cover with a damp towel and grow until doubled in bulk, 30 to 40 minutes, in a warm, draft-free place.

8. Preheat the oven to 375°F.

9. Melt two tablespoons of butter that were left. Brush the tops of the raised rolls with the melted butter using a pastry brush and bake for 18 to 20 minutes until they are browned on top.

6. Der Weiner Schnitzel's Chili Sauce

Preparation time: In about 45 minutes

Servings: 1

Difficulty Moderate

Ingredients:

- Two cloves garlic, minced
- Half cup of onion, minced
- Two tablespoons of olive oil
- One pound of ground beef
- One teaspoon of salt
- Half teaspoon black pepper
- One tablespoon of prepared mustard
- One tablespoon of vinegar
- One teaspoon of Worcestershire Sauce
- Half teaspoon Tabasco
- A quarter cup of ketchup
- Half cup of tomato juice

Instructions:

1. Cook the garlic and onion in a big, heavy skillet in oil over medium heat, stirring until the onion is softened.

2. Add beef and cook, stirring and using a fork to break up any lumps, until cooked through. Drain the extra fat away.

3. To make a thick and creamy loose but not soupy mixture, add the remaining ingredients, adding just enough juice.

4. Simmer the sauce, stirring regularly, for about 10 minutes.

5. For the top 6 hot dogs, make ample sauce.

6. Steam the hot dogs and use rolls of potatoes.

7. Olive Garden's San Remo Seafood Dip

Preparation time: In about 35 minutes

Servings: 1

Difficulty: Moderate

Ingredients:

- One (6 oz.) can of tiny shrimp (drain, reserve liquid)

- One (6 oz.) can of crab meat (drain, reserve liquid)

- Two oz. cream cheese, cubed

- Two tablespoons of olive oil

- Two tablespoons of flour

- A quarter teaspoon of salt

- 1/8 teaspoon crushed garlic

- One teaspoon of horseradish

- 1/3 C. asiago cheese

- Two tablespoons of grated parmesan cheese

- 3/4 C. half and half

- One and a half C. Barilla marinara sauce (remove excess liquid)

- A quarter C. parmesan cheese (for topping)

- breadsticks bought at the store

Instructions:

1. Heat the olive oil and flour in a two-quart saucepan over medium-low heat. From canned seafood, incorporate liquids.

2. Add the cream cheese cubes, salt, garlic and horseradish. Stir well until smooth. Add two teaspoons of parmesan cheese and asiago. Until smooth, stir.

3. Add seafood; combine well. Simmer until it is heated. Add half and a half to the seafood sauce a little at a time.

4. Simmer for 12-15 minutes. Stir occasionally, just don't scorch. Spray with a non-stick spray in a small baking dish.

5. Use this marinara to cover the bottom of the dish. Place the mixture of seafood on top of the marinara. Sprinkle the quarter C. of Parmesan Cheese. Bake for 10-15 minutes at 325F. Don't turn brown. Before serving, let it cool for a few minutes.

6. Now, for the breadsticks, follow the baking time and temperature directions on the box.

7. Brush them with olive oil and sprinkle them with Parmesan cheese before placing them in the oven. Tinfoil wrap.

8. When they are finished, cut them into dipping bits on a diagonal

8. Dave and Buster's Cheddar Mashed Potatoes

Preparation time: In about 25 minutes

Servings: 4

Difficulty: Easy

Ingredients:

Garlic Butter

- One teaspoon of minced garlic
- One tablespoon of olive oil
- Eight tablespoons (one stick) butter, softened
- One teaspoon of chopped fresh parsley

Potatoes

- Two pounds red potatoes, scrubbed and cut into 1-inch chunks
- 1/3 cup heavy cream
- Four ounces white Cheddar or Monterey Jack cheese, shredded
- Salt and pepper

Instructions:

1. By gently sautéing the garlic in the olive oil, make the garlic butter; it should be soft but not brown.

2. Add the softened butter and parsley, mix gently, dump into a covered container, and cool until ready to use.

3. In salted boiling water, cook the potatoes until they are tender, 5 to 10 minutes, then drain well.

4. Add the cream, cheese, and ¼ cup of the garlic butter and place them in a warmed serving bowl. With a hand mixer, mash with a fork or pound rather gently, then season with salt and pepper to taste.

9. Olive Garden's Gnocchi with Spicy Tomato and Wine Sauce

Preparation time: In about 1 hour

Servings: 8 to 12

Difficulty: Moderate

Ingredients:

- A quarter cup extra virgin olive oil

- Twelve cloves garlic, peeled

- A quarter teaspoon of red pepper flakes

- One tablespoon of chopped fresh basil, or One teaspoon of dried, plus extra for garnish

- One teaspoon of chopped fresh marjoram

- Two cups of dry white wine

- Two cups of chicken broth

- Two 28-ounce cans of whole tomatoes, diced tomatoes, or crushed tomatoes, with juice

- Eight tablespoons (one stick) butter, chilled, cut into pieces

- Half cup grated Parmesan cheese, plus extra for garnish

- Salt and black pepper

- Four pounds gnocchi, fresh or frozen, cooked according to the package instructions

Instructions:

1. In a large saucepan, heat the olive oil and sauté the garlic, red pepper flakes, one tablespoon of fresh basil and marjoram until golden brown.

2. Add the chicken broth and white wine and cook for about 10 minutes. Add the tomatoes and cook for another 30 minutes until the liquid is reduced by half.

3. Put half of it in a blender until the sauce is reduced, then puree it with the butter and half a cup of Parmesan cheese. Season with black pepper and salt.

4. With the chunky tomato mixture, return the pureed sauce to the saucepan and stir to blend.

5. In a serving bowl, place the warm gnocchi and coat it with the sauce. Use parmesan and basil to garnish.

10. Lawry's Creamed Spinach

Preparation time: In about 35 minutes

Servings: 8

Difficulty: Easy

Ingredients:

- 20 ounces frozen chopped spinach two packages

- Four slices of finely chopped bacon

- A quarter cup minced onion

- Four tablespoons of all-purpose flour

- Two teaspoons Lawry's seasoned salt

- One teaspoon of black pepper

- Three teaspoons of minced garlic

- Two cups of warmed milk

Instructions:

1. Cook the spinach according to the instructions given in the packet and drain well. When crisp, fried the bacon bits, set them aside. Remove most of the pan's bacon drippings.

2. Sauté the onion until very tender in the remaining pan drippings. Add bacon to the onion mixture and cook for some time.

3. It will be a thick paste roux to remove the onion/bacon mixture from the heat and stir in the flour, salt, pepper, and garlic and combine thoroughly.

4. In one step, add the warmed milk all in one. Return the mixture to medium heat, constantly stirring until smooth and thickened.

5. Add the spinach and thoroughly blend. Keep the finished dish hot until it is ready for serving.

11. Olive Garden's Italian Sausage–stuffed Portobello Mushrooms with an Herb and Parmesan Cheese

Preparation time: In about 45 minutes

Servings. 4

Difficulty: Moderate

Ingredients:

Cream Sauce

- Two cups of heavy cream

- A quarter cup grated Parmesan cheese

- Two tablespoons of chopped fresh basil, or two teaspoons of dried

- Salt and pepper

Stuffing

- Two large eggs

- 1/4 cup milk

- One teaspoon of chopped fresh Italian flat-leaf parsley

- One teaspoon of chopped fresh basil

- One teaspoon of chopped fresh marjoram

- One clove garlic, chopped

- One cup of finely ground garlic croutons

- A quarter cup grated Parmesan cheese

- One pound bulk Italian sausage

- Four large portobello mushrooms

- Fresh parsley sprigs or basil leaves, for garnish

Instructions:

1. Make the cream sauce first. Bring to a gentle boil the heavy cream and reduce it by half. Stir in a quarter cup of parmesan cheese, basil, salt and pepper. And put aside.

2. Make the stuffing ready. In a large bowl, whisk together the eggs, then add the milk and mix properly. Add the parsley, basil, garlic, marjoram, ground croutons, and 1/4 cup of the Parmesan cheese. And put aside.

3. In a skillet, sauté the sausage, breaking it up as it cooks. Remove it with a slotted spoon until it is completely browned, then add it to the stuffing mixture, stirring well to blend.

4. Preheat the oven to 350°F.

5. Remove the stems and the mushrooms' spongy undersides so that they resemble hollowed-out bowls.

6. Place them on a baking sheet, open side down, and bake for around 8 minutes, or until they are a little soft.

7. With the sausage mixture, stuff the mushroom caps and place them back in the oven to bake for 15 to 20 minutes, until golden brown on top and cooked through.

8. Spoon some cream sauce over each mushroom for serving and garnish with a sprig of parsley or fresh basil. Serve warm.

Chapter 12: Dessert Recipes

1. Subway White Chocolate Macadamia Nut Cookies

Preparation time: In about 50 minutes
Servings: 24 Cookies
Difficulty: Moderate

Ingredients:

- Half cup butter
- 3⁄4 cup sugar
- One egg
- One teaspoon of vanilla extract
- One and 1⁄4 cups of flour
- Half teaspoon baking soda
- Half teaspoon salt
- Eight ounces chopped white chocolate
- One (6.5-ounce) jar of chopped macadamia nuts

Instructions:

1. Preheat the oven to 375°F.

2. Cream the butter and the sugar together in a medium bowl. Stir in the vanilla and egg.

3. Stir in the creamed mixture and combine the flour, baking soda, and salt.

4. Stir in the nuts and chocolate.

5. Drop the cookies, approximately 2″ apart, by heaping teaspoonfuls on an ungreased cookie sheet.

6. Bake until lightly browned, for 8-10 minutes.

7. On wire racks, let it cool. When cool, store it in an airtight container.

2. Olive Garden Apple Carmelina

Preparation time: In about 55 minutes

Servings: 2

Difficulty: Moderate

Ingredients:

Topping

- 3/4 C. flour

- Five tablespoons of butter softened

- A quarter teaspoon of salt

- Half C. brown sugar

- A quarter C. sugar

Filling

- Two (20 oz.) cans of sliced apples, drained

- Half C. sugar

- Half teaspoons of apple pie spice

- A quarter C. brown sugar

- A quarter C. flour

- A quarter teaspoon of salt

Instructions:

1. Mix apples, Half C. sugar, apple pie spice, A quarter C. brown sugar, salt, and flour together, stir well.

2. Pour into an 8' x 8' baking dish that is finely buttered.

3. In a bowl, put the topping ingredients together. Integrate the flour, salt and sugar and blend well.

4. Add to add the topping ingredients to the softened butter. The mixture should look like a coarse meal.

5. Sprinkle over apples and put for 30 - 35 minutes in a preheated oven at 350F. Serve topped with a drizzle of caramel sauce and your desired vanilla ice cream.

3. Golden Corral Bread Pudding

Preparation time: In about 1 hour

Servings: 2

Difficulty: Moderate

Ingredients:

- Three cups of French bread cubed and partially dried
- Half cup of melted butter
- Two cups of whole milk
- Two eggs beaten
- One teaspoon of cinnamon
- A quarter teaspoon of salt
- 1/3 cup brown sugar (dark)

White Sauce

- One cup of whole milk
- Two tablespoons of butter
- Half cup of granulated sugar
- One teaspoon of vanilla
- One tablespoon of flour
- dash of salt

Instructions:

1. Scald together the milk and butter. Suspend and put aside.

2. Eggs are beaten, brown sugar and cinnamon are added. Add the egg mixture when the milk is cold enough to make sure the egg mixture does not curdle.

3. Add bread cubes, whisk thoroughly and do not beat. Place in a well-oiled 8"x11" skillet.

4. Place it for around 40 minutes in a preheated oven at 350 degrees F; check with a toothpick. Set aside when done.

5. Mix all ingredients for the sauce and bring to a boil for 3-4 minutes, stirring continuously. Set aside for 5 minutes, pour about half of the mixture over the warm bread pudding and put the sauce's remainder in a serving bowl for those who like the little extra.

6. Better served warm at room temperature.

4. Cracker Barrel Cherry Chocolate Cobbler

Preparation time: In about 1 hour

Servings: 2

Difficulty: Moderate

Ingredients:

- One and a half cups flour

- Half cups sugar

- Two teaspoons of baking powder

- Half teaspoon salt

- A quarter cups of butter

- One (6 oz.) package of Nestle's semi–sweet chocolate morsels

- A quarter cups of milk

- One egg

- One (21 oz.) can of cherry pie filling

- Half cups nuts, finely chopped

Instructions:

1. Preheat the oven to 350F. Combine the flour, sugar, baking powder, salt and butter in a wide bowl; cut with a pastry blender until the crumbs are the same size as the peas.

2. Nestle's semi-sweet chocolate morsels are next to be melted over hot (not boiling) water. Remove from heat and cool at room temperature slightly (about 5 minutes).

3. In molten chocolate, add milk and egg and mix properly. Blend the flour mixture with the chocolate.

4. Spread the bottom of two-quarters of the casserole with the cherry pie filling.

5. Drop the chocolate batter over the cherries randomly.

6. Sprinkle with nuts that have been chopped.

7. Bake for 40 – 45 minutes at 350 F.

8. With heavy cream, serve warm.

5. Olive Garden's Golden Cinnamon Orzo Calabrese

Preparation time: In about 40 minutes

Servings: 4

Difficulty: Moderate

Ingredients:

- ¼ cup walnut halves
- Eight ounces orzo pasta, cooked according to the package instructions
- One 12-ounce can of evaporated milk or evaporated skim milk
- Three tablespoons of sugar
- One tablespoon of ground cinnamon
- Half cup golden raisins or dark raisins
- ¼ cup prepared apple butter

Instructions:

1. In a shallow oven-proof skillet, place the walnuts and toast in a preheated 400 ° F oven. Bake until the nuts are a soft golden brown, sometimes flipping. (Or toast over low heat in a dry skillet, flipping often.) Let it cool, then chop.

2. Add the evaporated milk, sugar, and cinnamon and put the cooked orzo in a pot. Simmer until much of the liquid is absorbed, then extract from the heat.

3. Add the raisins, sliced walnuts, and apple butter and stir. Pour the mixture into small bowls when the ingredients are combined and ready for 10 minutes. Cover and refrigerate to serve it cold.

6. Applebee's Blondie Brownies

Preparation time: In about 45 minutes

Servings: 12

Difficulty: Moderate

Ingredients:

- One cup of flour
- Half teaspoon baking powder
- Pinch baking soda
- Pinch salt
- Half cup chopped walnuts

- 1/3 cup melted unsalted butter
- One and 1/3 cups of packed brown sugar
- One egg
- One tablespoon of vanilla extract
- Half cup of vanilla baking chips
- A quarter cup unsalted butter
- A quarter cup maple syrup
- One (8-ounce) package softened cream cheese
- Half teaspoon maple extract

Instructions:

1. Preheat the oven to 350°F.

2. Sift the flour, baking powder, baking soda, and salt together. Stir the nuts in. And put aside.

3. To beat the butter and one cup of brown sugar together, use an electric mixer.

4. Whisk in the vanilla and egg.

5. Beat the dry mixture into the wet mixture gently. Stir the vanilla baking chips together by hand.

6. Spread flour into a 9″by 9 ″by 2″ baking pan that is oiled. Bake for 20 to 25 minutes or until it comes out clean with a toothpick inserted in the middle. Set to cool aside.

7. Melt ¼ cup of butter and maple syrup over low heat in a saucepan. In the saucepan, stir the remaining 1/3 cup of brown sugar until it has dissolved.

8. Remove from the heat and beat the saucepan with the cream cheese and maple extract until smooth. Return the saucepan to low heat and boil until the peanut butter consistency, for roughly 5 minutes, then spread the mixture over the top of the cooled brownies.

7. Applebee's Strawberry Dessert Shooters

Preparation time: In about 40 minutes

Servings: 4

Difficulty: Moderate

Ingredients:

- One and a half (8-ounce) packages of cream cheese
- Two eggs
- 1/3 cup sugar
- Two tablespoons of sour cream
- Half teaspoon vanilla extract
- Half cup of graham cracker crumbs
- Two tablespoons of melted butter
- Half cup thawed frozen sliced strawberries in syrup
- Whipped cream for garnish

Instructions:

1. To make the cheesecake filling, combine the cream cheese, eggs, sugar, sour cream, and vanilla until smooth in a large bowl, using a blender.

2. Pour the mixture into a large saucepan and simmer for 8 to 10 minutes over medium-high heat, frequently stirring, or until the mixture starts to thicken.

3. Pour it into a covered container and freeze until cold for several hours.

4. Combine butter with graham cracker crumbs to prepare every serving.

5. In a 6-ounce glass, spoon two teaspoons of graham cracker crumbs and cover with 1/3 cup of the cheesecake filling.

6. Top with two tablespoons of strawberries and syrup on top of the filling of a cheesecake and finally whipped cream. Then serve.

8. Cheesecake Factory Oreo Cheesecake

Preparation time: In about 2 hours

Servings: 1 Pie

Difficulty: Hard

Ingredients:

- Two tablespoons of melted butter

- One and a half cups of Oreo cookie crumbs

- One and a half pounds room-temperature cream cheese

- One cup of sugar

- Five room-temperature eggs

- One cup of room-temperature sour cream

- ¼ cup flour

- Two teaspoons of vanilla extract

- ¼ teaspoon salt

- Fifteen divided coarsely chopped Oreo cookies

Instructions:

1. Preheat the oven to 375°F.

2. Combine the butter and cookie crumbs into a greased 10" pie pan and press uniformly into the rim. And put aside.

3. Use an electric mixer to pound the cream cheese until light and fluffy. Add the sugar and then the eggs. Incorporate the sour cream, flour, vanilla and salt. Stir in 5 chopped cookies.

4. Pour the mixture into the pan and cover with the remaining cookies that have been chopped.

5. Bake for 7 to 5 minutes on the top rack.

6. Turn off the oven, open the door and give 1 hour for the cake to rest in the oven.

7. Overnight, refrigerate.

9. Arby's Apple Turnovers

Preparation time: In about 40 minutes

Servings: 8

Difficulty: Moderate

Ingredients:

- Four large cooking apples
- Half cup sugar
- One tablespoon of cornstarch
- One teaspoon of lemon juice
- ¼ teaspoon ground cinnamon
- One (17.3-ounce) package puff pastry sheets
- Half cup confectioner's sugar
- One tablespoon of water

Instructions:

1. Firstly, peel, core, and slice the apples. Cook apples with sugar, cornstarch, lemon juice, and cinnamon in a medium saucepan over low heat, constantly stirring, for 6-8 minutes until the apples are tender. Freeze until cold.

2. At room temperature for 20 minutes, thaw the pastry sheets.

3. Preheat the oven to 400 degrees F.

4. On a finely floured board, unfold the pastry. Roll each sheet into a square of 12", then cut into four squares of 6".

5. Place in the middle of each square ¼ cup of apple mixture. With water, brush the sides. Fold and seal the edges tightly with a fork to form triangles.

6. Place on baking sheets and bake until golden, or for 25 minutes. On the wire rack, let it cool.

7. Mix the sugar and water from the confectioners in a little bowl for the sugar drizzle. Drizzle over the turnovers with a spoon and allow to set before serving.

10. Hostess Snowballs

Preparation time: In about 45 minutes

Servings: 2

Difficulty: Moderate

Ingredients:

- Four egg whites

- Half cup of butter

- One cup of sugar

- Half teaspoon vanilla extract

- Half teaspoon almond extract

- The rind of one lemon, finely grated

- Two cups of sifted cake flour

- One tablespoon of baking powder

- 2/3 cup milk

- Two to Three cups of sweetened shredded coconut

Frosting

- One (16 oz.) package of powdered sugar

- One (7 oz.) jar Jet-Puffed Marshmallow Creme

- A quarter cup margarine or butter softened

- One teaspoon of vanilla extract

- One to Two tablespoons of milk

Instructions:

1. To 350F, preheat the oven. Butter and flour the muffin tins or baking molds and set aside.

2. In a clean bowl, whip the egg whites until firm but not dry, and put them in the fridge while making the rest of the batter.

3. The butter is creamed, and the sugar is added. To blend, continue mixing.

4. Add the vanilla extract, lemon rind and almond extract and blend properly.

5. Sift the flour with the baking powder three times and then make three additions to the butter mixture alternately with the milk.

6. Fold in the whites and pour in the molds with the batter, filling up about 3/4 of the way. Bake for 20 to 25 minutes until the batter in the center is firm to the touch. Let the pans cool, then turn out so that the top becomes the bottom of the (you may need to trim them a bit so they sit flat).

7. Beat the sugar, marshmallow creme, margarine or butter and vanilla extract with an electric mixer at medium speed for frosting, beating the milk to the desired frosting consistency as desired.

8. For a pale hue, place the coconut in a bowl and add one drop of red or green food coloring.

9. Toss until the coloring of the food is well blended in and the perfect color is obtained. Frost the top and sides of the cakes to make them look like snowballs and dip/roll them in coconut.

11. Olive Garden Apple Carmelina

Preparation time: In about 50 minutes

Servings: 6 to 8

Difficulty: Moderate

Ingredients:

Filling

- Two (20-ounce) cans of drained sliced apples

- Half cup sugar

- Half teaspoon of apple pie spice

- 1/4 cup brown sugar

- ¼ cup flour

- ¼ teaspoon salt

Topping

- ¾ cup flour

- ¼ teaspoon salt

- Half cup light brown sugar

- ¼ cup sugar

- Five tablespoons of softened butter

Instructions:

1. Preheat the oven to 350°F.

2. In a bowl, put together all the Ingredients: for the filling and stir well.

3. Pour the mixture into an 8″ x 8″ baking dish that's also lightly buttered.

4. Adding the flour, salt, and sugars and blending well, create the topping in a separate bowl. Work in the butter. The mixture should look like a coarse meal. After, sprinkle over the apples and bake for 30 to 35 minutes.

12. Bennigan's Death by Chocolate Cake

Preparation time: In about 40 minutes

Servings: 6 to 8

Difficulty: Moderate

Ingredients:

- One (18.25-ounce) box chocolate cake mix

- One cup of Kahlua

- Four (3.9-ounce) boxes of Jell-O chocolate pudding mix

- Three (8-ounce) containers of Cool Whip

- Six Skor candy bars

Instructions:

1. For a 9″by 13″ cake, bake the cake according to the box instructions. With a fork, poke the top of the baked cake and spill the Kahlua over the cake.
2. Just let this soak in. It can be left overnight this way.
3. In compliance with the box instructions, make the chocolate pudding.
4. Crumble half of the cake to assemble the cake, and put it on the bottom of a large glass bowl. Layer half a sheet of pudding, then half of Cool Whip, half a layer of Skor's candy bars, broken into little pieces.
5. Repeat until all covered and then serve.

13. Pizza Hut Dessert Pizza

Preparation time: In about 1 hour

Servings: 8

Difficulty: Moderate

Ingredients:

- One (13.8-ounce) can of refrigerated pizza dough
- One (21-ounce) can of cherry, blueberry, or apple pie filling
- Half cup flour
- Half cup brown sugar
- Half cup quick oats

- Half cup cold butter

- One teaspoon of cinnamon

- Two cups of powdered sugar

- Three tablespoons of milk

- One tablespoon of butter

- One teaspoon of vanilla

Instructions:

1. Preheat the oven to 400 degrees F.

2. On a floured board, roll the dough until it is the pizza pan's diameter. Place the dough in the pan and mold it towards the edge.

3. Brush with vegetable oil and use a fork to prick.

4. For 3 minutes, prebake the dough, then take it out of the oven.

5. Over the dough, spread the pie filling.

6. Just use a fork or pastry blender to mix the flour, brown sugar, quick oats, cold butter, and cinnamon, and spoon over the filling.

7. Place the pizza back in the oven and commence to bake for 10-15 minutes or until a golden brown is in the crust. Afterward, remove from the oven.

8. By combining powdered sugar, milk, butter, and vanilla, create the vanilla drizzle. Pour the glaze over the pizza.

14. Bob Evans Peanut Butter Pie

Preparation time: In about 3 hours 15 minutes

Servings: 1 pie

Difficulty: Hard

Ingredients:

- One (5-ounce) package Jell-O instant vanilla pudding
- Two cups of cold milk
- Half cup whipped cream
- One and 1⁄4 cups of creamy peanut butter
- One pre-baked pie shell
- One (8-ounce) container Cool Whip
- Chocolate syrup, for garnish
- Crushed peanuts for garnish

Instructions:

1. In a bowl, whisk together the pudding mixture and milk until smooth. Add the peanut butter and whipped cream and whisk until completely combined.
2. With a generous coating of Cool Whip, pour into the pie shell and seal. Place in the freezer, until set, for 1 hour.
3. Remove and drizzle with your desired chocolate syrup and crushed peanuts from the fridge.
4. For 2 hours, cover and chill.

15. Starbucks Black Bottom Cupcakes

Preparation time: In about 45 minutes

Servings: 36 cupcakes

Difficulty: Moderate

Ingredients:

- One (8-ounce) package softened cream cheese

- 1/3 cup sugar

- One large egg

- Pinch salt

- Two cups of semisweet mini chocolate chips

- Three cups of flour

- Two cups of sugar

- 2/3 cup sifted unsweetened baking cocoa

- Two teaspoons of baking soda

- Half teaspoon salt

- Two cups of water

- 2/3 cup oil

- Two tablespoons of white vinegar

- Three teaspoons of vanilla

Instructions:

1. Preheat the oven to 350°F. Line 36 muffin tins of standard size with paper liners.

2. Beat the cream cheese, sugar, egg, and salt in a bowl until they are soft and well mixed. To blend, put in the chocolate chips and mix. And put aside.

3. Sift flour, sugar, cocoa, baking soda, and salt together in a bowl.

4. Whisk the water, oil, vinegar, and vanilla together in a small bowl. Beat well until mixed thoroughly.

5. Combine the wet and then dry ingredients.

6. Fill 3/4 of the liners with chocolate batter and drop about one teaspoon of the cream cheese mixture on top of each chocolate batter and in the middle.

7. Bake for about 20 minutes or until the test for the cupcakes is done.

16. Cheesecake Factory Pumpkin Cheesecake

Preparation time: In about 2 hours

Servings: 1 Pie

Difficulty: Hard

Ingredients:

- One and a half cups of graham cracker crumbs
- Five tablespoons of melted butter
- One cup of plus One tablespoon of sugar
- Three (8-ounce) softened packages of cream cheese
- One teaspoon of vanilla
- One cup of canned pumpkin
- Three eggs
- Half teaspoon cinnamon
- ¼ teaspoon nutmeg
- ¼ teaspoon allspice
- Whipped cream for garnish

Instructions:

1. Preheat the oven to 350°F.

2. Combine the graham cracker crumbs, butter, and one tablespoon of sugar in a medium bowl. Stir good enough to coat the butter with all of the crumbs.

3. Press the crumbs onto the bottom and up the sides of a 9" pie pan about two-thirds of the way. For 5 minutes, bake the crust. And put aside.

4. Combine the cream cheese, one cup of sugar, and vanilla in a large mixing bowl. Mix until smooth with an electric mixer.

5. Pumpkin, eggs, cinnamon, nutmeg, and allspice are added and then start beating until creamy and smooth.

6. Into this pan, pour the filling. For 60-70 minutes, bake. At this point, the top will get a little darker. Take the cheesecake from the oven and allow it to cool.

7. Place it in the fridge until the cheesecake has reached room temperature.

8. Serve it on top with a nice amount of whipped cream.

17. The Melting Pot Flaming Turtle Fondue

Preparation time: In about 35 minutes

Servings: 2 to 4

Difficulty: Moderate

Ingredients:

- Two ounces melted milk chocolate

- Two ounces caramel sundae syrup

- Whole milk for thinning, if necessary

- 1/3 ounce of 151 rum

- One ounce of chopped pecans

Instructions:

1. In a saucepan, heat the chocolate and caramel over low heat, stirring regularly.

2. If the mixture is too thick, add the whole milk slowly to achieve the best consistency.

3. Add the rum to the pot slowly.

4. By touching the flame to the pot's edge, carefully ignite the liquor using a long match.

5. Add the nuts to the pot and mix until the flame burns out.

18. Taco Bell Caramel Apple Empanadas

Preparation time: In about 45 minutes

Servings: 12

Difficulty: Moderate

Ingredients:

- One (12-ounce) package of Stouffer's frozen harvest apples

- One tablespoon of flour

- ¼ cup butter

- ¼ cup firmly packed light brown sugar

- ¼ teaspoon ground allspice

- Three and a half cups of baking mix

- One cup of whipping cream

- Two tablespoons of melted butter

Instructions:

1. Preheat the oven to 400 degrees F.

2. Thaw the apples for 6–7 minutes at half power in the microwave. For 3 minutes, make them stand. With the flour, stir together.

3. Melt half a cup of butter over medium heat in a medium skillet. Add the mixture of apples, brown sugar and allspice. Cook, constantly stirring, for 4 minutes or until the mixture thickens. Suspend from the heat.

4. Mash the apple mixture coarsely and set aside.

5. Stir together the baking mix and whisk the cream until moistened with a fork. On a well-floured surface, turn out the dough and knead 3-4 times.

6. Roll the dough to a thickness of ½" and cut it into 12 squares (5").

7. Divide the apple mixture into 12 servings and in the middle of each square, place one serving.

8. Fold over the square on one side, pressing the edges with a fork to secure. Place on a baking sheet that is lightly oiled. With melted butter, brush the tops and bake for 18-20 minutes or golden brown.

19. Chili's Mighty Ice Cream Pie

Preparation time: In about 3 hours

Servings: 1 pie

Difficulty: Hard

Ingredients:

- One Oreo cookie crust
- One (6-ounce) package Heath Bits
- One cup of semisweet chocolate chips
- Half gallon vanilla ice cream
- 1/3 cup chocolate fudge topping
- 1/3 cup caramel topping

Instructions:

1. Separately, freeze the pie crust, Heath pieces, and chips. When bits and chips of Heath are frozen, chop them until perfect in the food processor. Put the bits in the freezer again.

2. Just until it is workable, soften the ice cream so that the pieces can be stirred in without melting the ice cream.

3. In a chilled mixing bowl, put the thawed ice cream and add Heath bits and chocolate chips that have been processed. Stir and blend well.

4. Place the ice cream in the frozen shell of the pie and chill for 2 to 3 hours. In two separate bowls, place 1/3 cup of chocolate fudge topping and 1/3 cup of caramel sauce and melt both bowls on medium heat in the microwave for 1–2 minutes until moderately melted.

5. Lift the pie from the freezer, line the pie with chocolate and caramel sauce, and put it back in the freezer. Before serving, freeze for 2–3 hours.

20. Just-Like Entenmann's Raspberry Cheese Danish

Preparation time: In about 55 minutes

Servings: 2

Difficulty: Moderate

Ingredients:

For the Pastry

- Two tubes crescent roll dough

- One egg white

For the Filling

- One package (8-ounce) cream cheese, softened

- ¼ cup of sugar

- One whole egg

- Half teaspoon vanilla

- ¼ cup seedless raspberry preserves

For the Glaze

- Half cup confectioner's sugar

- One to two tablespoons of fresh lemon juice

- One teaspoon of lemon zest

Instructions:

1. Preheat the oven to 350°F. Spray a 13 x 9-inch baking pan or gently oil it.

2. Prepare to fill, except the raspberry preserves, by beating all filling Ingredients: together.

3. Open one of the crescent roll dough tubes and split it into two rolls in the middle of the roll (on the perforation). Unroll each segment. Two rectangles are what you will have.

4. Place one rectangle in half of the pan, and replicate at the other end of the pan with the other half of the dough. Pat in the pan, forming a bottom crust and sealing the perforations as best you can.

5. Spread the filling with cheese on top of the crust. Dot up the raspberry preserves and scatter over the top of the cheese filling as best you can (it doesn't matter if it's sloppy).

6. Open the other crescents and repeat the above process, splitting the middle perforation into two rolls.

7. Unroll each into a rectangle and put it on top of the cheese/raspberry filling as you did with the crust. Try to close the perforations as well as cover the whole top, as best you can. Again, it does not matter if it's a little messy.

8. Brush the top with the egg white.

9. Bake for 30-35 minutes at 350 degrees F, or until the top crust is golden brown. Remove and cool absolutely after taking out from the oven. Chill for around 2 hours as desired.

10. To make a pourable glaze, prepare the glaze by combining the sugar, lemon zest and one tablespoon of lemon juice at a time. Drizzle the Danish top with the glaze.

11. Refrigerate any portions left.

21. Starbucks Oatmeal Cookies

Preparation time: In about 50 minutes

Servings: 36 cookies

Difficulty: Moderate

Ingredients:

- One and a half cups of old-fashioned oats
- Half cup flour
- ¼ cup dark raisins
- ¼ cup golden raisins
- ¼ cup dried cranberries
- ¼ teaspoon baking powder

- ¼ teaspoon baking soda

- Half teaspoon salt

- Six tablespoons of room-temperature butter

- Half cup packed dark brown sugar

- ¼ cup sugar

- One large egg

- Half teaspoon ground cinnamon

- One teaspoon of vanilla

- Four tablespoons of dark raisins for topping

- Four tablespoons of golden raisins for topping

Instructions:

1. Preheat the oven to 350 degrees F

2. Oats, flour, raisins, cranberries, baking powder, baking soda, and salt are mixed. And put aside.

3. Whisk together the butter and sugar until light and fluffy. Add the egg, vanilla, and cinnamon and beat until blended.

4. Add the oat mixture to the butter mixture steadily. Beat before they're mixed.

5. In a different bowl, blend and set aside the raisins for the topping.

6. Drop the dough onto two thinly greased baking sheets with rounded tablespoons, 2'' apart.

7. On top of the dough, place one rounded teaspoon of raisins.

8. Bake until the cookies are golden brown but still soft, around 12-16 minutes.

9. Cool on sheets before serving.

22. Chili's Molten Lava Cake

Preparation time: In about 55 minutes

Servings: 4

Difficulty: Moderate

Ingredients:

- Five tablespoons of butter

- Three and a half ounces dark chocolate

- Two extra-large eggs

- One extra-large egg yolk

- Three teaspoons of sugar

- One teaspoon of vanilla extract

- Three tablespoons of flour

- Two teaspoons of cocoa powder

- One teaspoon of salt

Instructions:

1. Preheat the oven to 425 degrees F.

2. For 2-3 minutes on medium heat, melt the butter and chocolate together in the microwave. Stir to blend.

3. Whisk together the eggs, sugar and vanilla in a large mixing bowl until the mixture is bright yellow and the sugar is dissolved.

4. In the egg mixture, stir the warm chocolate mixture and whisk until mixed. Sift in the flour, salt and cocoa. Until paired, fold in with a spatula.

5. Spoon into four 5-ounce buttered ramekins, and tap to settle any air bubbles on the surface.

6. For 30 minutes, refrigerate.

7. Put the ramekins in a baking dish and add water to the dish until it's halfway up the sides.

8. For 15 minutes, bake and then serve.

23. Cracker Barrel Carrot Cake

Preparation time: In about 45 minutes

Servings: 1 sheet cake

Difficulty: Moderate

Ingredients:

- Three cups of flour
- Two teaspoons of baking powder
- Two teaspoons of baking soda
- Half teaspoon salt
- Two teaspoons of ground cinnamon
- One teaspoon of ground nutmeg
- Half teaspoon ground cloves
- One and A quarter cups of vegetable oil
- One and a half cups of sugar

- Half cup brown sugar
- Two teaspoons of vanilla
- Three eggs
- One cup of crushed pineapple
- 3/4 cup finely chopped walnuts
- Half cup shredded coconut
- Two cups of shredded carrots
- Half cup raisins
- Cream Cheese Frosting
- Eight ounces cream cheese
- Half cup room-temperature butter
- One teaspoon of vanilla
- Two cups of powdered sugar
- Half cup chopped pecans for garnish

Instructions:

1. Preheat the oven to 350°F.

2. Mix the flour, baking powder, baking soda, salt, nutmeg, cinnamon and cloves together. And put aside.

3. Mix the oil, sugar, vanilla, and eggs in a large bowl, using a beater, until smooth and fluffy. Mix, then incorporate the pineapple, walnuts, coconut, carrots, and raisins. Add the flour mixture half at a time progressively until it is mixed through.

4. Pour the batter into a 9″by 13″ oiled and floured tray and bake for between 40-50 minutes. Test for doneness with a toothpick.

5. Blend the cream cheese and butter until it is light and smooth for the frosting. At the same time, add vanilla and a little powdered sugar until it is well combined.

6. Turn the mixer up and beat until it is light and moist with frosting.

7. Over the cooled cake, spread the frosting and sprinkle with pecans.

24. Cracker Barrel Banana Pudding

Preparation time: In about 40 minutes

Servings: 6 to 8

Difficulty: Moderate

Ingredients:

- One and a half quarts of milk

- One and ¼cups of liquid egg substitute

- One and 1/8 cups of flour

- ¼ cup vanilla extract

- One and ¼cups of sugar

- ounces vanilla wafers

- One and ¾ peeled bananas

- One (8-ounce) container Cool Whip

Instructions:

1. In a saucepan, heat the milk to 170°F.

2. Blend the eggs, flour, vanilla, and sugar in a bowl.

3. In the pan, add the sugar mixture to the milk.

4. Cook until it becomes custard-like for 10-12 minutes, stirring continuously.

5. Spread on the bottom of the baking tray with the wafers.

6. Slice and put the bananas over the wafers.

7. Over the wafers and bananas, pour the custard.

8. Let cool and add Cool Whip to the top before serving.

25. Waldorf Astoria Red Velvet Cake

Preparation time: In about 1 hour

Servings: 16

Difficulty: Moderate

Ingredients:

Cake

- Half cup shortening
- Two eggs
- Two ounces red food coloring
- One cup of buttermilk
- One tablespoon of vinegar
- One teaspoon of baking soda

- One and a half cups sugar

- Three tablespoons of cocoa

- Two and A quarter cups of all-purpose flour

- 3/4 teaspoon salt

- One teaspoon of vanilla

Frosting

- Three tablespoons of all-purpose flour

- One cup of milk

- Half cup shortening

- Half cup butter

- One cup of sugar

- One teaspoon of vanilla

Instructions:

1. Preheat the oven to 350°F.

2. Take three cake pans and dust with oil and flour.

3. Create cocoa and food coloring paste.

4. In a bowl with cream shortening, eggs, and sugar, add the mix of cocoa and food coloring. Mix thoroughly.

5. Add buttermilk with vinegar and flour with salt alternately.

6. Fold in vanilla with baking soda by hand.

7. Pour batter into cake pans in similar proportions.

8. Bake at 350 F for 30 minutes or until it comes out clean with a toothpick inserted in the middle.

9. Remove the layers of cake from the pans and let it cool.

10. Cook the flour and milk until thick to make the frosting.

11. Beat shortening, sugar, margarine, vanilla until smooth.

12. Add the combination of milk and flour a little at a time and stir well.

13. Pour it over the cake, let cool and serve.

26. Olive Garden Strawberries Romano

Preparation time: In about 40 minutes

Servings: 4

Difficulty: Moderate

Ingredients:

- One cup of mascarpone cheese

- 1/3 cup brown sugar

- Juice of one orange

- One tablespoon of triple sec

- One cup of whipped cream

- Two quarts quartered strawberries

- Fresh mint sprig

Instructions:

1. Combine the cheese, brown sugar, orange juice, and triple sec in a mixing bowl and blend thoroughly. Fold the whipped cream over it.

2. In a dessert dish or wine glass, place the berries. Top with a mixture of cream.

3. Garnish with a mint sprig and chill before ready to be served.

27. Chili's Chocolate Chip Paradise Pie

Preparation time: In about 2 hours

Servings: 1 Pie

Difficulty: Hard

Ingredients:

Crust

- Three tablespoons of butter
- 1/3 cup graham cracker crumbs
- Three tablespoons of sugar
- 1/3 cup chocolate chips

Filling

- Half cup flour
- ¼ cup sugar

- ¾ teaspoon baking powder

- 1/3 cup milk

- One tablespoon of oil

- One teaspoon of vanilla extract

- 1/3 cup semisweet or milk chocolate chips

- ¼ cup shredded coconut¼ cup crushed walnuts or almonds

- Two tablespoons of butter per slice of pie

- Dash of cinnamon

Toppings

- Ice cream

- Hot fudge and caramel toppings

Instructions:

1. Preheat the oven to 350°F.

2. For the graham cracker crumbs and sugar, heat the butter and mix.

3. In a 1-quart casserole bowl, press the mix into the rim. Cover uniformly with the chocolate chips and bake until the chocolate is molten for 5 minutes. Spread out uniformly over the crust with the molten chips.

4. Combine the dried ingredients in a large mixing bowl. Add the milk, vanilla, and oil and whisk until it is creamy. Stir in the coconut, chocolate chips, and nuts.

5. Pour into the crust and bake until a toothpick inserted into the middle comes out clean, uncovered, for 35-40 minutes.

6. On an ovenproof serving tray, to serve, put two teaspoons of butter and then sprinkle with cinnamon. Place the butter in a warm oven until it melts.

7. Remove the plate from the oven and put the melting butter directly on a large slice of warm pie.

8. Top the pie with ice cream and drizzle with caramel toppings and hot fudge.

28. Outback Steakhouse Key Lime Pie

Preparation time: In about 4 hours

Servings: 1 Pie

Difficulty: Hard

Ingredients:

Crust

- One stick butter

- One cup of graham cracker crumbs

Filling

- One cup of water

- Three cups of sugar

- One package unflavored gelatin

- One teaspoon of salt

- Juice of three limes

- One cup of condensed milk

Instructions:

1. Melt the butter in a skillet to cook the crust. Mix the crumbs in. Press it into a 9″ pie pan.

2. Heat the water, sugar, gelatin, salt, and lime juice in a pot to prepare the filling. Without boiling, add the condensed milk and heat for 5–7 minutes.

3. Into the crust, pour the filling and let the pie cool. Cool for 4 hours in the refrigerator.

29. The Melting Pot Dark Chocolate Raspberry Fondue

Preparation time: In about 35 minutes

Servings: 2 to 4

Difficulty: Moderate

Ingredients:

- 12 ounces finely chopped dark chocolate

- ¼ cup heavy cream

- Three tablespoons of raspberry liqueur

Instructions:

1. In a microwave-safe bowl, combine the chocolate and cream.

2. Heat for 2–3 minutes in the microwave on medium heat, stopping to stir after 30 seconds. Better take note not to make the chocolate burn.

3. Pour into a pot of warm crock or fondue.

4. Drizzle the liqueur with it. Suggested dippers contain graham crackers, marshmallows, and fruit.

30. Applebee's Chocolate Sin Cake

Preparation time: In about 1 hour

Servings: 2

Difficulty: Moderate

Ingredients:

- Two tablespoons of butter

- Six oz. semisweet chocolate

- Two oz. bitter chocolate

- One C. unsalted butter

- One teaspoon of vanilla extract

- Four eggs, at room temperature

- Four egg yolks, at room temperature

- Half C. brown sugar, firmly packed

- Six tablespoons of corn starch

- Ten oz. package of frozen red raspberries in a heavy syrup, thawed

- One pint of fresh raspberries

- Twelve triangular cookies or chocolate pieces

- Twelve sprigs of fresh mint

Instructions:

1. Butter (or coat with no-stick cooking spray) twelve 4-oz sides and bottoms of ramekins and put aside.

2. Combine the semi-sweet chocolate, bitter chocolate, butter and vanilla on top of the double boiler over the simmering water. Stir to mix and set aside until the butter and chocolate are melted.

3. Combine the eggs, egg yolks, and brown sugar in a broad mixer bowl and beat on high for 5-7 minutes or until dense and quadrupled in thickness.

4. Reduce to low speed and add cornstarch, one tablespoon at a time, beating with each addition to incorporate. Increase to high speed and beat for 5 minutes or until soft peaks are contained in the mixture.

5. Fold the chocolate into the egg mixture with a rubber spatula, scratching the bowl's bottom and sides frequently. Divide batter into prepared ramekins and bake for 10 minutes in a preheated 375-degree F oven (cake will be lightly crusted with a soft center). Remove from the oven and let it cool.

6. Cover and refrigerate with plastic wrap until ready to eat, then loop a knife blade along the cake's sides to remove the cake from the ramekin. On a serving tray, invert the ramekin.

7. Lift the ramekin, leaving the cake in the middle of the tray. In a mixer, pour the thawed raspberries and puree. Strain the seeds and discard them.

8. Spoon the cake with raspberry coulis and garnish with fresh raspberries, triangular cookies or a bit of chocolate and mint.

Chapter 13: Beverages Recipes

1. Galiano

Preparation time: In about 10 minutes
Servings: 4
Difficulty: Easy

Ingredients:

- Two Cup Sugar

- One cup of Water

- A quarter teaspoon of Anise extract

- One teaspoon of Vanilla extract or Vanilla Bean Extract

- Three Drops of yellow food coloring

- One-Fifth vodka

Instructions:

1. In a pan, combine sugar and water and bring it to a boil. Boil it for 1 minute and reduce the heat immediately. Simmer for 1 hour or until the mixture thickens. Remove and cool from the heat.

2. Pour sugar-water syrup into a quart-size sterilized bottle.

3. Add the extract of anise, vanilla and food coloring. Gently whisk and add vodka.

4. Cover and let the mixture rest before serving for ten days to 2 weeks.

2. Olive Garden Sangria

Preparation time: In about 20 minutes

Servings: 1 gallon

Difficulty: Easy

Ingredients:

- 1.5 Liters Soleo Red Table Wine

- oz. Grenadine

- oz. cranberry juice cocktail

- oz. sweet vermouth

- oz. sugar water (5 oz. sugar diluted)

- Strawberries, oranges, and crushed ice

Instructions:

1. Mix all ingredients in a big deep glass or bowl, except for ice.

2. Pour sangria into a glass and then add ice and fruit.

3. Orange Julius

Preparation time: In about 25 minutes

Servings: 4

Difficulty: Easy

Ingredients:

- Six ounces orange juice, from frozen concentrate, unprepared

- One cup of milk

- One cup of water

- A quarter cup of sugar

- One teaspoon of vanilla

- Eight ice cubes

Instructions:

1. Combine all ingredients of the drink, except ice cubes, in a blender.

2. In a blender, blend for about 1–2 minutes, adding ice cubes one at a time, until smooth.

4. Harry's Bar Bellini

Preparation time: In about 20 minutes

Servings: 1

Difficulty: Easy

Ingredients:

- One peach (white peach if available)

- Six ounces champagne chilled

Instructions:

1. Wash the peach properly.

2. Then core the washed peach and peel it and puree it in a blender.

3. In a champagne flute, add one tablespoon of the puree and finish it off with champagne, swirl and serve.

5. Chili's Presidente Margarita

Preparation Time: in about 45 minutes

Servings: 1

Difficulty: Easy

Ingredients:

- One and a quarter ounces Sauza Commemorative Tequila, anejo tequila
- Half ounce Presidente Brandy, or your favorite brandy
- Half ounce orange liqueur Cointreau, or your favorite orange liqueur
- 4 ounces sour mix
- Splash of lime juice
- Margarita salt

Instructions:

1. Cut the lime into the wedges
2. Rub a lime wedge around the rim of the Margarita glass
3. Dip wet glass rim into Margarita salt and fill the glass with ice
4. In a cocktail shaker, add tequila, orange liquor, Brandy, sour mix, ice and shake until blended
5. Strain and pour over the ice in the Margarita glass

6. Applebee's Banana Berry Freeze

Preparation time: In about 25 minutes

Servings: 2

Difficulty: Easy

Ingredients:

- Two cups of ice

- One peeled ripe banana

- 3⁄4 cup strawberry daiquiri mix

- 1⁄4 cup piña colada mix

- Whipped cream for garnish

- Strawberry slices, for garnish

- Banana slices, for garnish

Instructions:

1. Purée ice, banana, daiquiri, and colada mix in a blender on high until the mixture is smooth.

2. Pour into two wine glasses.

3. Garnish with whipped cream, strawberries, and bananas.

7. Bennigan's Candy Bar Drink

Preparation time: In about 15 minutes
Servings: 1
Difficulty: Easy

Ingredients:

- One and ¼ ounces Frangelico

- Two ounces chocolate syrup

- Two ounces Coco Lopez

- Two ounces finely shredded coconut

- Two ounces of ice milk

Instructions:

1. Combine all the ingredients in a blender.

2. Serve in champagne or other small glass.

8. Chili's Calypso Cooler

Ready in about: In about 25 minutes

Servings: 1

Difficulty: Easy

Ingredients:

- One and a half ounces Captain Morgan spiced rum

- Half ounce peach schnapps

- Four ounces of orange juice

- Splash lime juice

- Half ounce grenadine

- Orange wedge, for garnish

- Maraschino cherry, for garnish

Instructions:

1. Fill a 16-ounce glass with ice.

2. Pour all of the ingredients of the drink over ice in the order listed. Do not stir.

3. Garnish the drink with an orange wedge and a cherry on a toothpick.

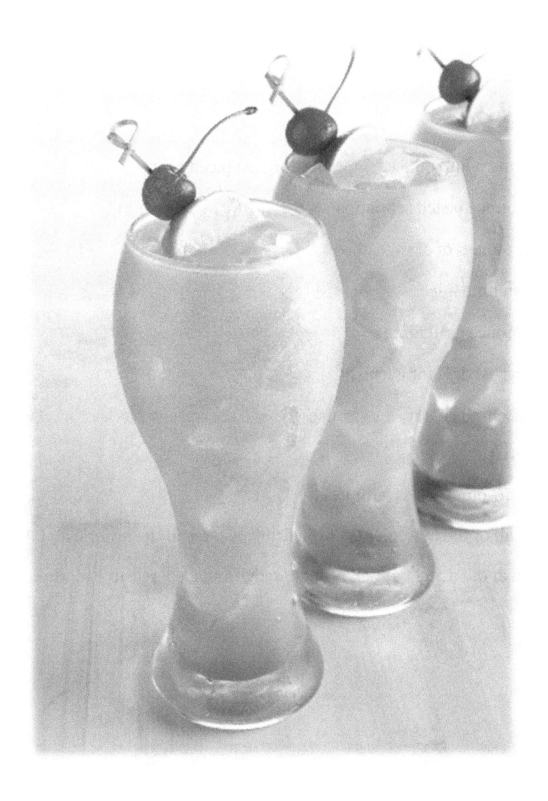

9. Chili's Electric Lemonade

Preparation time: In about 20 minutes

Servings: 1

Difficulty: Easy

Ingredients:

- One and 1⁄4 ounces Bacardi Limon vodka

- Half ounce Blue Curacao

- Two ounces sweet and sour mix

- Splash of 7-Up

- Lemon wedge, for garnish

Instructions:

1. Put vodka, Blue Curacao, and sweet and sour mix in a shaker with a lid.

2. Mix well. Pour into a glass.

3. Add the splash of 7-Up and garnish with a lemon squeeze.

10. Outback Steakhouse Wallaby Darned

Preparation time: In about 25 minutes

Servings: 2

Difficulty: Easy

Ingredients:

- Eight ounces of frozen sliced peaches

- Half cup Bacardi Fuzzy Navel mix

- Half cup ice

- Half cup champagne

- Three ounces of water

- One and a half ounces peach schnapps

- One and a half ounces vodka

- One tablespoon of sugar

Instructions:

1. Place all the drink ingredients into a blender.

2. Blend until smooth.

3. Pour into 2 (10-ounce) glasses and serve immediately.

11. T.G.I. Friday's Chocolate Monkey

Preparation time: In about 25 minutes

Servings: 1

Difficulty: Easy

Ingredients:

- Half ripe banana

- Two scoops of vanilla ice cream

- One scoop of crushed ice

- One ounce banana liqueur

- Half ounce chocolate syrup

- Whipped cream for garnish

- Banana slices, for garnish

- Cherry, for garnish

Instructions:

1. Place all the drink ingredients into a blender. Blend until thick and creamy.

2. Serve in a tall wine glass with a straw. Top with whipped cream.

3. Garnish with banana slices and a cherry.

12. T.G.I. Friday's Flying Grasshopper

Preparation time: In about 25 minutes

Servings: 1

Difficulty: Easy

Ingredients:

- ¾ ounce of green Crème de Menthe

- ¾ ounce of white Crème de Cacao

- ¾ ounce of vodka

- Two scoops of vanilla ice cream

- Half scoop crushed ice

Instructions:

1. Combine all the ingredients in a blender. Blend until smooth.

2. Serve in tall specialty glass.

13. Tommy Bahama Millionaire Mojito

Preparation time: In about 15 minutes

Servings: 1

Difficulty: Easy

Ingredients:

- Two parts Tommy Bahama White Sand Rum

- One teaspoon of superfine sugar

- Juice of one lime

- Crushed ice

- Dash of sparkling soda

- One bunch of fresh mint

Instructions:

1. In a shaker, mix the rum, sugar, and lime juice. Add ice.

2. Shake well and pour into a glass that is chilled.

3. Add sparkling soda.

4. Garnish with a sprig of mint.

Conclusion

I'm very thankful that you took the time to read this book. I hope that all your queries are clear with regards to Copycat recipes.

Cooking a Copycat Recipe is not different from cooking food at home. All you need to know is the ingredients and techniques the chef uses while cooking those famous and popular dishes.

It is a cost-effective method of enjoying the famous dishes you like with ease at your dining table in your home. It is not a tiresome process, but you need to be patient enough and persistent to make and savor those restaurant dishes without spending extra bucks in the comfort of your home.

Keep cooking and keep experimenting with the recipes.

Thank you, and good luck!

CPSIA information can be obtained
at www.ICGtesting.com
Printed in the USA
BVHW062344010621
608546BV00013B/2010

9 781914 129742